YOU ARE NOT

L ive a small life? I cannot. And neith. that raised Jesus Christ from the dead lives in each one or us. ... given us that life-changing power so that we are able to do the very thing He has placed us on the earth to do.

Then why do we feel a sense of restlessness? I believe it is because deep down we know we were made for more than where we are and what we are doing right now. There is something to be birthed through us. Whatever our history has been we know we are somehow a part of destiny and we want to play our part in realizing that.

God gave us more than our own gifts, talents, and abilities. He gave us more than inspirational quotes and motivational pep rallies. He gave us His very self in the person of the Holy Spirit so that we would never be limited to achieve only what is possible on our best day.

Jennie, thank you for bringing us to this because it is to our Father's Glory that we bear much good fruit during our brief sojourn on this earth. And dear reader, I pray that you dream big, believe big, and dare big during your one and only life on this planet. Impossible is where God starts and miracles are what God does. Go on, I dare you to let God be God in you so he can be God through you!

CHRISTINE CAINE
AUTHOR OF *UNDAUNTED*

T hey say the world is made up of individual atoms. But the truth of it is that the world is made of individual stories. In the beginning was the Word—not atoms—and that very Word exhaled and breathed you into being and every story connects to another story that is changing the story of time—His Story.

Now is *your* story, and you and your story matter beyond time.

Now is your space on stage. Now is your time and now you are here for such a time as this. You will not pass by this way again. There is only one now. Eternity is worth the risk. Now is not the time to be demure with the gifts you've been given. Share them lavishly. Now is the time to let your life be poured out as ink in an epic story of bold sacrifice and startling courage. Now is the time to live upside down. Herein is rest for our restless souls.

There is a darkness that tries to spread the disease of "be big." Christ whispers the cure to the ego's disease: Decrease so I can increase. There is a lie that tries to convince that giving yourself for the world is what really matters. Christ is the Truth who whispers that giving yourself for one person is how you really change the world.

ANN VOSKAMP
AUTHOR OF *ONE THOUSAND GIFTS*

I keep hearing this common tension among women. It's funny because we are a generation that is so advantaged. We have more than our parents have—most of us have more schooling, bigger houses—we have every privilege, luxury even, and advantage. We've been given so much, and we are so blessed, and yet I keep hearing over and over, "I'm restless. I don't know what it is, I don't know what more I could possibly want, what am I missing? How could I still feel at all dissatisfied with this happy beautiful life that I've been given?"

I love it because I know that God is calling us deeper and deeper into the kingdom where things like houses and salaries and success simply cannot satisfy. He has set this longing in our hearts for more of Him, more of the gospel, more of His goodness, more of the kingdom, and so we find ourselves at this interesting crossroads as people of privilege who have been given much. But like Jesus told us, to whom much has been given, much will be required.

The life that God has set in front of us is exciting, and adventurous, and risky. Sometimes it's even dangerous. And it's going to ask everything of us, because apparently it doesn't care much for our comfort or our happiness or our safety, and yet it is the kingdom that satisfies. It is the gospel that makes us whole and gives us purpose.

My deepest hope for these years we have on this planet is that collectively we reach across and grab each other's hands and chase after God together. Where we're willing to risk anything for it, or sacrifice anything for it. I think that is the secret to this life. That's the secret to this kingdom Jesus was always trying to explain to us in the gospel. I believe it is worth it, and it is precious. So if you feel restless you are not alone. Let's join hands and chase after God together.

JEN HATMAKER
AUTHOR OF *SEVEN*

RESTLESS

RESTLESS

BECAUSE YOU WERE MADE FOR MORE

JENNIE ALLEN

W PUBLISHING GROUP

AN IMPRINT OF THOMAS NELSON

Published in Nashville, Tennessee, by W Publishing, an imprint of Thomas Nelson.

Thomas Nelson titles may be purchased in bulk for educational, business, fund-raising, or sales promotional use. For information, please e-mail SpecialMarkets@ThomasNelson.com.

Library of Congress Control Number: 2013914161

ISBN 978-0-8499-4706-3

Printed in the United States of America

14 15 16 17 RRD 6 5

"YOU HAVE MADE US FOR YOURSELF, O LORD, AND
OUR HEART IS RESTLESS UNTIL IT RESTS IN YOU."
—SAINT AUGUSTINE

GOD, YOU ARE HOME TO ME.
TAKE THESE WORDS AND LIGHT FIRES
THAT CANNOT BE PUT OUT—
FOR YOUR FAME ON THIS EARTH IN OUR TIME.

CONTENTS

PART 3: LIVING ON PURPOSE

PART 1

THE CALL

CHAPTER 1

A CALL TO DREAM

As I stared at the ceiling, I saw the scrape marks. Right after we had moved into our first house, Zac, my husband, scraped off the popcorn-textured ceiling. You'd think that would be something you'd never really notice—the ceiling—but it was something I stared at every afternoon. I stared as my newborn son slept. I had nowhere to be. Nothing to do.

I would lie on my beige sofa and stare at the marks that had been left in, trying to make something perfect of it. And in the quiet, surrounded by everything I thought I'd ever wanted, I felt that everything I'd ever wanted was strangling me.

I loved my family, but in the process of making a family I had somehow lost myself. Passions were pushed aside, dreams had trickled away, and the needs of other people outside my family had escaped me. My entire former life had been shut down for the immediate demands of one little person. I wondered if it was wrong to care about anything or anyone outside of these four walls. I wondered if I would feel permission to dream again.

I didn't need to find a career or even a calling. I had one. Motherhood. What I needed was a sense of purpose. I felt restless.

Was this feeling pushing me toward something bigger, or crippling me from loving the life I was given?

Maybe it was both.

Something in me still feels restless.

As we stare at the marks on the lives we have tried to make perfect, we ache a little.

The word *calling* has always seemed to tease me, like a mysterious secret containing the answer to my ridiculously restless spirit. We wonder if we are missing some mystical, great, noble purpose that was supposed to squeeze into the holes of our ordinary lives.

We feel numb.

We feel bored.

Let's assume that if we are breathing, then we have a purpose for being here. Every one of us with breath in our lungs still has something left to do.

I want to dream of what our purposes may be.

The conviction to write this book was born out of conversations with many of you. Since I wrote the first book, *Anything*, the most consistent thing I have been asked is some version of this question:

"I am in. I am all surrendered to God. But now what? I don't know what he wants me to do."

Every single one of us is designed to fit into a unique space with unique offerings. God's will for every one of us will look different. There is a framework within the commandments of Scripture, and within it we are free to create lives reflecting God and his passions here.

As I have wrestled with calling and purpose and dreaming this year, I have fallen deeply in love with the life of a man who surely lived restlessly in Scripture. Joseph's story, told throughout Genesis 37–50, is the story of a life that at times felt wasted, and yet God was working in every moment that felt mundane and unfair and dark, moving all of the mess into his unique purpose and calling.

This is a book about God.

And this is a book about us and God. And this is a book about the moment we close our eyes and see God. This is a book about facing the God of the universe and answering to him about the life and resources he gives us while we are here.

And because I think we all want that moment to go well, this is a book about discovering ourselves and getting over ourselves all at the same time. This is a book about being brave enough to imagine a better world, and how we may be used to make it that way. This is a book about changing the world and changing diapers. This is a book about fears and suffering and joy and gifts. This is a book about all that lies in our control and how nothing is in our control. This is a book about vision and obedience.

I feel a weight.

An indescribable burden.

A holy, God-given passion burning in my soul for you, for us, for our time here. Because I know we will blink and be together with God forever and there is life to be lived here, in our generation, on this earth, with our breath.

So I humbly ask you, dream with me.

We will lay out the unique threads of our lives that feel random, potentially even tangling us up, but we will lay them out and dream about eternal purposes for seemingly mundane moments and consider that it is possible to waste our lives.

And then let's not.

I'm not good with catchy titles. I just name projects based on how I feel . . . so here it is—here is what I feel, and I have a hunch I am not the only one:

Restless . . . because you were made for more.

I believe this is from God, and I pray it will spark something in you . . . a vision, perhaps, of the unique reason God keeps issuing you breath.

I want to dream of what our purposes may be.

I am going to ask you to join me in what might be a very uncomfortable process: I want you to dare to believe that God has a vision for how you are to spend your life. Because finding and accomplishing this vision is quite possibly the greatest responsibility we have as a generation, second only to knowing and loving God.

I wish I could promise magical moments with angels scripting visions in the sky just for you. I wish I could promise that at the end of our time together, you would never feel empty, numb, or bored again. I can't. But if you go here with me—I think we will see God move.

We have a call to dream.

The Old Testament described a day in the future about which God said:

> I will pour out my Spirit on all people.
> Your sons and daughters will prophesy,
>> your old men will dream dreams,
>> your young men will see visions. (Joel 2:28)

God promised a day would come when his people would be filled with his own Spirit. And when they were full of God, God himself would give his people dreams and visions.

Dreams and visions.

This day has happened. The Holy Spirit flooded the earth at Pentecost, and immediately after, Peter reminded them of the promise of that day:

No, this is what was spoken by the prophet Joel:

"In the last days, God says,
    I will pour out my Spirit on all people.
Your sons and daughters will prophesy,
    your young men will see visions,
    your old men will dream dreams." (Acts 2:16–17)

We live in the last days. We are filled with the Spirit of God, and we're living on this earth for relatively few days to accomplish the will and work and wonders of God. Why do we do this? So that "everyone who calls on the name of the LORD will be saved" (Joel 2:32).

Our creative God has an infinite number of creative plans to make himself known through us, his image bearers, so he sent his Spirit to give unique visions to unique people to reach the world in unique and beautiful ways.

The Spirit of God has dreams for you.

And he has given you an abundance of gifts, resources, people, and vision to accomplish *his* dreams for you. If you do not feel that way yet, you will.

What if?

What if the things you love to do collided with the plans God has laid out for you from before the foundations of the earth?

What if the random relationships and activities in your life all of a sudden had a focus and felt intentional and meaningful?

What if the things that have caused the most hurt in your life became the birthplaces of your deepest passions?

What if you could get past your fears and insecurities and spend the rest of your life running your guts out after his purposes for you?

The beige sofa upstairs is unthinkably dirty with the stains of over a decade of beautiful messy life; my quiet, sleeping baby turned into four big kids; and my minutes are overflowing now, filled with it all. Life. But I still feel it sometimes . . . a whisper of more. Not more because what I am doing isn't important, but because I so rarely believe that it is.

May this be the place where your restless soul meets God, and where dirty, beige sofas become beautiful, and where no life or minute or breath ever feels small again.

CHAPTER 2

TANGLED THREADS

I was unusually empty and didn't have the patience to give a funny opening illustration to cut the tension. With scripted notes in my hand and fifty women staring at me, expecting a typical church retreat in the middle-of-nowhere Texas, I paused. And in the space of that silence, I saw the same look in their eyes that I knew was in mine.

What was I going to do—follow the script? I sat in a room full of women who were hurting, doubting, numb, tired, insecure; and their teacher was feeling all the same things. What was supposed to happen here?

> *I sat in a room full of women who were hurting, doubting, numb, tired, insecure; and their teacher was feeling all the same things.*

I set down my notes.

I was struck with the idea that the lot of us may never be in the same room again this side of heaven, and, overwhelmed with the need I saw in front of me, I opened with these words:

"We have a little bit of time together—how about we just get after it? How about we really deal with our sin and hurt? How about we fight to find God here? And then let's dream about how we display God while we are on earth for a few years."

And I am almost certain everyone was looking at me, thinking, *No, seriously girl, where's the funny story?*

But then something happened. God's Spirit blew in and, with their eyes cutting across the room, hoping maybe it was safe enough, the women slowly let words fall out.

"I honestly don't care about God."

"I don't think God cares about me."

"I am afraid what people will think."

"I want a comfortable life."

"My spouse won't be on board."

"I think I will fail."

"I have nothing to give God."

"I don't think my life even matters this much."

Then, with all the mess of it pooling on the floor of our cabin, I looked around the room and saw a hint of something—a little sparkle, possible hope in their eyes.

Maybe this isn't life, I thought. *These thoughts can't be from God.*

The worries that had consumed each person moments before all of a sudden looked miserably ridiculous staring back at them. The realization needed no words to help form it. We were faced with a simple, striking image: strong, resourced, rescued people, full of God, going through life completely shut down by lies and fear.

Could it be possible there is more to life than this?

We were all certain that there was, and with all the chains on the floor, we could almost taste what we had been missing. We were about to remember what running with abandon felt like, what purpose felt like, what dreaming felt like, what freedom felt like.

Do you need to remember that there is more?

How to run freely?

What purpose feels like?

What freedom feels like?

Some of us have decorated our prison walls so beautifully that we have altogether forgotten we are sitting in a cell, wasting our lives. We don't know there are chains that, though they no longer bind us, still seem to tangle us up. We sit and listen to talks or read books about God, and we wonder why nothing changes when we so desperately want it to.

WHERE STORIES ARE BUILT

When I saw *Batman Begins* for the first time, I kept punching my husband's arm because I was coming out of my skin. I was so moved, so inspired. (*Batman Begins*, in Christopher Nolan's Batman trilogy, is hands down one of the best films on planet Earth.) A young Bruce Wayne watches as his parents are shot and killed, and he spends the next decade of his life seeking revenge, wandering the world as a restless, unsatisfied, lost soul and committing crimes. Bruce is insanely wealthy, trained, and gifted, but he has nothing to live for—no focus, no drive other than pain.

I picture his life as a bunch of loose threads: his pain, his wealth, his potential, his training, his gifts, the fate of his city blowing around in the wind as he tries to escape his pain. These are threads he wishes he could cut—they have no semblance of order or purpose; they seem to be entangling him, certainly not empowering him.

I picture his life when I look into most people's eyes. They have a similar look to them—hungry, unsettled, slightly unsure. But you can see in others only what you have tasted yourself.

Somewhere in the chaos of Batman's search, the threads of his life begin to untangle and weave themselves into something new.

Something potentially epic. Bruce can't escape the great pain and need screaming all around him in his home city of Gotham, so despite his reluctance and suffering, the threads of his life somehow bind together and equip him to meet that great need. The need finds him. Ironically, his purpose is woven together with the very threads that seemed to entangle him.

Ironically, his purpose is woven together with the very threads that seemed to entangle him.

Out of Bruce Wayne's deepest tragedy, fear, and pain—Batman is born.

Every one of us has a version of this same story in us. Some of you are thinking, *Yes, Jennie. I always think to myself, "Batman and I have so much in common."*

For the rest of you, here is where all of our stories converge:

You have threads of life blowing around, possibly even strangling you—threads that are meant to bind together and become your unique, God-given contribution to a world in great need. And not just for a world in need, but our souls were made to find their home in God with God's purposes for our life.

ACHING FOR PURPOSE

No unique purpose for your life will fill your soul. The only thing that will fulfill and settle your soul is God himself.

I am writing while neck-deep in the midst of what some may think is a great purpose. Zac and I are running hard toward God and doing our best to complete the works he is putting in our path for us to do for him. We are doing our best to raise our kids to love God and not be little punks. Zac is leading a church full of people who are hurting, and he spends most of his days looking people in the eyes and listening to their needs. I am writing and speaking the things God has given me to say. On some days, our threads seem to be meshing into something useful. I have never felt more peace and more joy, and yet life has never been more difficult.

Like today, for instance, I fight a deep desire to shut down this work, crawl back into bed, and live like this isn't important. I still feel restless. I struggle to keep pace with God, and I still fight my sin.

That's how I *feel* today. Now let me tell you what I *know*.

Our God is real.

Our God is coming.

Our God has plans for us.

Our lives are short.

We must get after it.

Because heaven is coming fast.

And what we are about to do here *is urgent*.

You have threads of life blowing around, possibly even strangling you—threads that are meant to bind together and become your unique, God-given contribution to a world in great need.

It's more urgent than we could ever imagine. We get to play little parts in the epic story of a God who put this whole universe in motion with a word.

> IF I FIND IN MYSELF A DESIRE WHICH NO EXPERIENCE
> IN THIS WORLD CAN SATISFY, THE MOST PROBABLE
> EXPLANATION IS THAT I WAS MADE FOR ANOTHER WORLD.
>
> C. S. LEWIS

Figure out what it means to run after God. Throw off what is holding you back. Find and live your part in his story. *That* is what we are going to do here in this journey together. And if ten of us do the work, it will all be worth it. Our generation could mark this earth and stamp it with the brand of a God who we all decided was worth it.

We tend to think that if we can land on our perfect purpose for our lives, we will finally be satisfied. Hear me: we have complete access to joy and purpose right now. Even with no grand vision from God, we have access to our Creator, and he is not hiding happiness from us. He gave it to us in the form of Christ. Everything we are going to talk about is just a response to our God. Our mattering doesn't depend on a stellar performance. We matter because we are children of the living, breathing, reigning God of the universe. We matter because we were bought with the blood of the Son of our Father God. He set us in our spots and in our time. He numbered our days and counts our hair. And we matter because he says we matter. This isn't a book about you suddenly finding a secret way to matter; it's about realizing you *already* matter, and therefore you can deeply desire to make your few days here count in light of all that is ahead for us as children of such a God.

I've wasted a lot of my life. I grew up with a sickening chase to win people's approval that I could not ever catch. And so I have given most of my life to the cause of being liked. God was never enough for me.

> We have complete access to joy and purpose right now.

It's not a noble cause. It's embarrassing, and I am sorry, because you probably were deeply hoping you picked up the book of a saint. You picked up the book of a sinner— likely a sinner worse than you. But chances are you aren't noble either, and likely you have wasted your life on . . . something.

But what if we just stop? What if we wake up? We are building mansions on sand when an enormous, steadfast, unmovable rock sits right beside us. This is why I will not put down my work and crawl into bed today, and I will stay and speak these words to you. Because for years I ran after uncatchable wind and built homes on sand, until I finally noticed that wind never stops escaping us and sand never stops shifting.

After a childhood observing a God I didn't need, at seventeen years old, I stood in front of three crosses at Kanakuk Kamp. I looked up at them and wondered at my own crimes, which had always seemed small until that moment. I looked at the crosses, and at the Jesus I had heard about all my life, and it occurred to me that I hung him there. I did it with my heart that loved people more than God—my heart that was black from building monuments to my reputation. I was haunted by pride and self, captivated with it all, bound by invisible chains heavier than the ones this world shames.

I saw my sin, and God saved my soul. And now all of us who love God are in it together, fighting to stay free and to free people around us, because there is a God who never escapes us and never shifts. Because people's eyes seem to contain similar hurt as mine did everywhere I go.

Is God real?

Do I matter?

Is there more than this?

Is this all worth it?

Yes. I swear it.

CHAPTER 3

DIE TO LIVE

My friends and I have a secret hobby. We sneak into Al-Anon meetings, although none of us have alcoholic relatives. But friends, there is a secret well of life in there. Raw need that has lost all the coverings of pretense. It feels like church, or how church should feel. Before you get all judgmental, hear me out. We go because we all have something happening in our lives that we cannot control. We go because Al-Anon doesn't tell you the truth—Al-Anon *shows* you the truth.

We listen to a tangled-up, beautiful mother striving to control her addicted, abusive, grown son, while she paces as if she were the guilty party, certain there is an answer—a way to change him. No one speaks, but we're clearly thinking in unison, chanting like a haunting chorus that won't leave your head, *Let go. Let go. Let go.*

We stay quiet, listen, and remember what we have all intellectually accepted since first encountering the red words of Jesus in children's church: "I say to you, unless a grain of wheat falls into the earth and *dies*, it remains alone; but if it dies, it bears much fruit. Whoever loves his life loses it, and whoever hates his life in this world will keep it for eternal life" (John 12:24–25 ESV, emphasis added).

The kind of life I want so badly lies on the other side of death.

A seed comes from the living flesh of a fruit. But it will never be more than a hard nuisance that gets stuck in our teeth, unless it is buried in the ground. And even then, in the dark, it is encased with a thick shell—dead and hard. But under the dirt, at some point, flesh is birthed out of something lifeless. It breaks through and pushes to the surface; it moves and grows, running up and out of something that was dead. Now it's alive—now it brings life.

We see in the striving of a tired mother what a thousand sermons whisper but never change in me: I can't let go, because it requires a little death. I know that tightening my grip will strangle what I'm holding, but I'm afraid of the sting that little death will produce.

But the kind of life I want so badly lies on the other side of death.

The kind of life you want lies on the other side of death.

I never noticed the hope in it at all until my heart was completely his. Before we begin to dream, there is one foundation that must exist: *surrender.*

We are going to dream God's dreams here. Maybe you picked up this book with some idea of what you hope to dream about—a small business or a noble cause to save the world—and we will get there. But as Bill Bright, the founder of Campus Crusade for Christ, used to teach, until there is surrender, there is no vision.[1] And Proverbs says, "Where there is no vision, the people perish" (Prov. 29:18 KJV).

We hurt for vision and direction from God. In another book,

Anything, I wrote about Zac and me praying a prayer of surrender. It's not an easy subject or an easy way of life. In fact, it costs us everything. We hand over every dream for our lives—every hope, every remnant of control we think we have—to God, and we say, "You have all of it. You have me. I am yours. Anything you want to do with me. Anything. I am in."

It's a terrifying thing. But it is essential before we begin. We were bought with an enormous price, and it is no longer we who live, but Christ who lives in us.[2] So, if we don't begin with surrender, we inevitably dream with vanity, with ego, with control.

The scariest and safest thing I have ever done is pray this prayer—to hand complete control of my life and my dreams over to my God. We all have hopes of how our lives will turn out, and we all fear that if God actually has his way with us, he may slingshot us to Africa or, worse, ask us to share Christ with the person in the house or cubicle next to ours. We are scared that God's dreams may not be as cool as the ones we create in our minds for ourselves.

Those of us who have been saved have been set apart for a great purpose—and that great purpose is actually not a secret: we are to know God and make him known. So we do not dream independently, and God does not sign off on our dreams. He is the builder of our dreams. We bring him our blank canvases, hand them over, and say, "Whatever you must create to display your glory, do it."

The words take my breath away, because there are days since that prayer when we have felt launched from his slingshot. Since we prayed that prayer, our lives have almost completely changed; but the scariest, most seemingly out-of-control moments have turned into our most favorite parts of life. From adopting our son from Rwanda to job changes, and reluctant moves to restoring strained relationships, each act of obedience felt like a small death. But each has turned out to breathe life into us in ways we couldn't imagine.

I do not ask you to pray for surrender lightly. We begin this process as every creator begins, with a blank canvas, hoping that something beautiful is about to come into being. But I have to tell you, there have been days when I have seen God painting pictures through our lives that I would give anything to paint over with my own brushstrokes. But we can't know what the picture will turn out to be. Like any great artist, we have to be open to the mystery of inspiration: God creating something through us.

> Until you are all in, you will only be capable of dreaming your own inadequate and small dreams. Because we are never free until we let go.

One of the most basic human questions we all ask is: "What is God's will for my life?"

We are going to have so much fun answering this question. *But* until you are all in, you will be capable of dreaming only your own inadequate and small dreams. Because we are never free until we let go.

That question, "What now?" makes me remember my own struggle to let go, and the way God rushed in when I finally did. From *Anything*:

> Most of my life I was looking for God to lead me loud and clear as he had for Mary with the angel. I had listened to sermons and read books about how to know the will of God. And with one simple, sincere prayer, he came flooding out of the woodwork as though he had been just waiting for this all my life. In the days to come, as I processed this, God started clearly bringing to life scriptures I had read a hundred times.
>
> Through these scriptures God was explaining to me,
> *Jennie, you hear me now so loudly and clearly because . . .*
>
> "I am the LORD, that is my name;
> my glory I give [or share] to no other." (Isa. 42:8)

And that is what you have been asking me to do until now. To share my glory. And I knew, Jennie, that

> "no servant can serve two masters, for either he will hate the one and love the other, or he will be devoted to the one and despise the other." (Luke 16:13)

So I was waiting. I was waiting to be the only thing. As with Martha, when I was in her living room while I was here in the flesh.

She was worried and upset about many things, but only one thing was needed. Mary had chosen the good portion, and it would not be taken away from her (Luke 10:41–42).

Mary had chosen me above every other thing—nothing was more important to her than me. Nothing mattered here but me.

When the rich man wanted me but wasn't willing to do anything, I had to show him he still loved something more, that he had another master, so I told him,

> "You lack one thing: go, sell all that you have and give to the poor, and you will have treasure in heaven; and come, follow me." (Mark 10:21)

And he wouldn't. He left me. He chose this life. See, I don't compete.

I was waiting, Jennie, calling you. I was waiting for you to see that while you wanted me all of these years, you had another master. Your heart was divided. You loved something else more, and I will not share my glory. I had to become your one thing . . . your only thing.

And so now . . . you will be hearing from me a little more.[3]

I want to let you into my reality. I write to you today beside the hospital bed of my best friend. My closest "everyday" friend in Austin has spent the last month in the ICU. We are all waiting to see if God will spare her life here or if he will take her home. It's unthinkable . . . three beautiful young kids and in the midst of a difficult divorce. So this project is set amid dark days. I long for comfort in this life, perhaps more than I ever have. So if you feel too weary to dream—if you feel too empty to give—you have good company. But with the ache for "easy" comes a whisper of bigger things. It feels impossible to write trite words beside this hospital bed.

Sarah has had multiple massive strokes over the last several days.

Will she live?

And if she does live, will she ever be the same?

These are the wrestlings of my soul with our God today:

Today we wait as fears toss around in our heads—fears that we dare not speak.

God, evil bows to you and yet it seems to be flooding us. And this darkness bends to somehow reflect your glory, but oh, the cost feels so high.

I walk in the front doors of the hospital several times a day. I walk past a small statue that I've never noticed the dozens of times I have bounced in to see new moms with their healthy babies. It's an image of you. You are draped on a cross with nails holding you there.

We keep looking at the darkness, and it feels like you messed up here . . .

Maybe you forgot she has a two-year-old who won't remember her. You forgot she is the best mom, and her kids adore her and need her. You forgot she's already suffered enough and depends on you for her every breath. You forgot she makes us all laugh more than any other friend we have. You forgot that so many people love her that we can't all fit in waiting rooms.

Or is it us who's forgetting?

Maybe we forget that we see days and you see eras. We see a friend and you see your child. We see sickness and death and you see our never-ending, unimaginable future life. We see a waiting room in mourning, and you see Sarah and me in ten thousand years, laughing and cutting up together at your table. We see three children without their mama and you hold their souls and see just how to press into them.

You get to be God whether we like it or not. You get to decide how this goes, and we can only beg at your feet. And when you seem forgetful to me . . . .

> *Great people do not do great things; God does great things through surrendered people.*

I walk past the statue and you yell to me from your cross:

I have forgotten nothing. And I am not passive about my approach to this problem.

I deal. I deal with this sickness and pain and death.

I do not forget. I bleed out for this.

So as you walk past me on that cross, Jennie, into a room that feels out of control and full of suffering, don't see a weak, distant, forgetful God.

You see a God who tells oceans where to stop and a God who tells evil where to stop.

You see a God who bleeds out for those you hurt for.

You see a God who suffered first. I AM with you.

And I have a plan here.[4]

Hear me: whatever he does with our lives, he is good and is fighting for us in the most noble ways; he gave his Son's life to win us back. So might he pour our lives out in difficult ways? Yes. But he is the God of planets and my soul. He gave everything for us. So I will entrust my entire life to no one else.

We surrender to a God who surrendered everything for us.

This is the joy set out before us and offered now. A union with the God of the universe, who passionately rescued us from ourselves and to himself. I trust him. He came down from heaven to get to us. He is worthy of our surrender. How ridiculous for me to want to paint my own story.

Great people do not do great things; God does great things through surrendered people. If I breathe here for a few decades, I would rather lose everything temporary for anything that is permanent.

We make a beautiful exchange:

Our short lives for forever.

Our moving sand for the rock of a God who adores us.

Our chains for running wild and free.

Our unsatisfying wind for the substance of a purpose that will never fade.

And as I look at my best friend, I wonder, *How do we possibly dream right now?* I wonder how we can go on this journey when she can't, and how we can enjoy this luxury when she can't move or speak.

But then I get barely a glimpse of our lives ten thousand years from now, and I realize I'm asking the wrong questions. How can we not?

As much as I want an umbrella drink by an ocean somewhere, I just as much want to never waste a minute.

With my mind that works and my fingers that type and my body that moves and my life every bit as thin as Sarah's—we get to dream. We get to live our lives worthy of the most amazing calling. As much as

I want an umbrella drink by an ocean somewhere, I just as much want to never waste a minute.

Because if Sarah leaves us now to go to Jesus, and I follow in a few more decades, it will feel like we were all here for just a little while.

So, can you pray "God, anything. You have me"? If so, this is about to get fun.

CHAPTER 4

PERMISSION TO DREAM

The word *dream* used to contain some poetic magic when we were children. Dreaming possessed our minds. We dreamed that eggplants were really plants that make eggs, and being a policeman was the perfect profession because they shoot real guns, and fairies were very interested in teeth and built castles with them somewhere. And we couldn't wait to fall in love and close our eyes and kiss a boy for the very first time at our wedding, which would have periwinkle-blue cupcakes and dresses and flowers.

God is a dreamer too. He built universes and generations of people out of his dreams. And God built us to dream.

dream (n.)
> A strongly desired goal or purpose.

Something that fully satisfies a wish.
A visionary creation of the imagination.[1]

Dreaming strips life of borders and sometimes of its reality and damage. Eventually we realize there are limits, and dreaming digresses to the pastime of children. Then most of our imaginations evolve into problem-solving mechanisms. Because eventually enough of our dreams don't come true that we just stop bothering.

None of us will ever get over watching Fantine in *Les Miserables*, with every dream in pieces on the floor of the slums. It's an infamous hopeless moment. Death is coming for her, and she sings these words:

> *I had a dream my life would be*
> *So different from this hell I'm living*
> *Now life has killed the dream I dreamed.*[2]

But that was not the end of this story. There were dreams bigger than the ones life killed.

Some moments in childhood you remember because of decrepit old photos, and some moments your parents have relived an inordinate number of times. But a very few moments you remember because your soul was just utterly and completely satisfied.

I was nine and it was Christmas Eve, and all my cousins and aunts and uncles had packed our little house to an uncomfortable level. Dad usually read the Christmas story, but this year he pulled me aside and asked me to take all the cousins in the back to act it out. Leading twenty little people at such a task with no adult assistance should have overwhelmed a nine-and-a-half-year-old. But instinctively I knew what to do. I knew what parts kids would play, I knew what each person should wear and say, and I managed to gather that army of toddlers and small children and create something beautiful and meaningful and funny.

I remember a room of uncles and aunts and grandparents cracking up as my little one-year-old sister was pulled out in her walker to announce the birth of Jesus, complete with a gold, pipe-cleaner halo and one of Dad's white undershirts covering the walker. That moment is sealed with pictures and stories.

But then Christmas was taken down, and I was still nine and our house was tame again. I was sitting on the floor of our living room, running my hands through our beige shag carpet all by myself. There aren't pictures or funny stories to remind me of this moment. But I vividly remember sitting on the floor and reliving my Christmas production over and over in my mind. I wanted to feel that satisfied again—to vision-cast and create and lead. Okay, I didn't use those exact words in my head. But my nine-year-old mind chased dreams of becoming a director and making movies in Hollywood. I can still imagine myself sitting with my hands in the carpet, picturing the cameras and lights and me orchestrating a grand production.

I was nine, and I wasn't dreaming about being famous or important or even mattering. I didn't care yet about all of that. I was just purely and perfectly dreaming of using my gifts, my life, to create something bigger than myself.

We were built with the ability to dream, but we've lost it.

What did you dream about as a kid?

What did you want to be when you grew up?

When did you stop dreaming?

I remember dreading adulthood. Becoming like my parents. I was eighteen and passionate and flitting to and from hostels in Europe, last-minute parties with friends around campfires in some likely illegal spots, and internships in Washington that didn't pay. I dreamed about changing the world; it all felt possible and, honestly, like no big deal. But most of us grow up at some point.

The first time I was introduced to the infamous Bob Goff, he was bouncing up and down on the stage at the 2012 Catalyst conference with a photo up behind him of the little boy suspended by balloons. Bob wrote a book of simple tales of a life lived based on love and dreams, *Love Does*. He lives with whimsy, and nothing on earth is out of his reach. If he can think of it, it is possible—no big deal.

We all used to be that way. But we have lost our whimsy. Our dreams have died, and in our pursuit of maturity, we have lost ourselves and even lost more of God.

MISSING GOD

I sometimes feel guilty for dreaming. Is this selfish? Shouldn't we just focus completely on God and not get narcissistic, thinking there are "special" things we should all be doing? Just focus on God?

It is honestly a good thing to think about, because we live in a time in church history where we have strategically justified obsessive amounts of self-focus. We have made life about our little stories rather than God's story. We have become a generation obsessed with understanding ourselves, as if that holds the answer for our restless, discontent souls.

We have come to treat God as if he exists for us, rather than us existing for him.

We have come to treat God as if he exists for us, rather than us existing for him. As if he is supposed to fit our plans, rather than our only plan being to know him and to follow him.

God is big, but he moves into the small. God cares about eternity, yet he cares about every second of every human's life. That is who we serve. When God is *only* big and *only* about eternal heavenly things in our minds, we miss out.

We miss Jesus.

We miss that Jesus loved each individual deeply and met their unique needs. We miss how creatively he pursued each of us until we believed. We miss his vision for his church: one body, many unique parts coming together to make a difference with their small moments.

We miss his Spirit.

Jesus ascended and sent a helper to live in and through us, to pray for us, to equip us with unique gifts, to encourage us, and to remind us of our purpose here. We miss this beautiful, personal interaction with our living God, if God only stays the distant Creator of planets in our minds. Jesus promised to give us himself in a very useful form—a form that would invade us and pour through us, comfort and equip us, and remind us that we are headed to a home better than the one we will risk for him now.

We miss God's creativity.

Just look around. You look different than the other people around you. Everything about you is different than every other human on earth. By design.

He stretches out eternity and stretches out the foundations of this earth, and then he comically thinks to stretch out the neck of a giraffe. He creates generations and billions of interesting humans, and then he takes the time to write intimate and unique moments for each one of them.

Ignore this side of God, and you will miss the point: he ran after you. He wrote stories for you. He numbered your days. He knows your thoughts before you think them and your words before you speak them. Ignore that he adores you and you might as well go ahead and shrivel up and die and go to heaven to be with him. He is big, and he moves into the small. It's God's dichotomy that makes him so absolutely mind-blowing.

We miss the mystery of God.

My favorite professor in seminary taught me the most painful and difficult truth about following God: *embrace the tension.* Because if you don't, you will land somewhere wrong about him.

I watch online as religion bloggers and theologians all fight for various values they hold dear. They are fighting on some deep level for what they believe is absolutely true of God. But often in the fight, they pull so hard (God is *this way* and not *that way*) that they yank away the tension that maintains truth. Even humans can't be easily boxed in. I've had friends call me melancholy, and others think I am over-the-top passionate. But both sides are true at times, and they are not in opposition to each other. If humans can't be completely boxed in, God certainly can't be either.

Part of good theology is learning to embrace tension and mystery. I've studied God deeply in personal and intellectual ways, and I have only more questions than when I started. Somehow, in his holy otherness, our God is:

- sovereign and has given us the freedom to make decisions;
- loving and just;
- the one who hates evil, and yet has full authority over it and permits evil's existence;
- one God and yet three all at once;
- the one for whom time doesn't exist, and yet he intentionally planned every moment of it for us.

And I could go on all day long.

We hate tension. We love to land somewhere, but this one little admonition—*embrace the tension*—keeps me humble, keeps God God, and keeps me slightly capable of knowing a smidgen of him. He is unknowable in so many ways, so mystery must be applied to our small understanding of him and what he has revealed to us in

Scripture. But we do know, through his Word and his Spirit, that he has given us enough. "His divine power has given us everything we need for a godly life" (2 Peter 1:3).

We often desperately chase knowledge of "God's will for me" at the sacrifice of God's will. We will not do that here. Let's embrace the tension of seeking God's will for us, individually, within God's revealed will for this earth—for eternity and for his people. We won't ever stop searching for purpose until God's will becomes our passion.

This one little admonition—embrace the tension—keeps me humble, keeps God God, and keeps me slightly capable of knowing a smidgen of him.

What could cause us to miss his plans for us? I think a lot of us are afraid, and some of us have deep needs that we don't even have words for. Before we go any further, let's start thinking about what those needs might be.

CHAPTER 5

UNCERTAINTIES

I was feeling brave that day, and a little fed up with the thoughts holding my mind captive. I was dipping my toe into dreaming, but I hadn't spoken any of the dreams aloud.

"I am feeling so restless . . . I think that perhaps there is more that God wants for me."

I vulnerably uttered these words over coffee with a friend. I was aching to dream with her that day. I wanted to wonder aloud if there could be any hint that it was God moving me with this unsettled feeling. Maybe he was, and maybe he wasn't. But I deeply wanted to find the answer to the question that had haunted me for years and seemed to be growing. She listened to me mumble clumsy thoughts, and she saw hints of God in my wanderings.

She even mentioned that, but with her every mention of freedom to dream was a warning: "But . . . be sure."

Every mention of the Holy Spirit followed with the words, "But . . . be sure Scripture takes priority."

Every mention of a restless feeling followed with the words, "But . . . be sure you aren't just being ungrateful for all you have been given."

For every mention of potential callings outside of my home with young kids, "But . . . be sure your kids come first."

For every mention of using gifts that may become more public, "But . . . be sure you don't promote yourself."

And as a zealot of a person, I hate the words, *But . . . be sure*. They give me flashbacks of the tension I felt as a child, when I was finally old enough to go exploring in the woods behind our house. Exhilaration and freedom flooded me as I ran out the back door, and just as all that energy was launched forward, my mom pulled me back, issuing a list of rules and boundaries beginning with the words, *But . . . be sure*. I couldn't have cared less in that moment about her list of rules; I'd already caught a whiff of hope and freedom and adventure. I wanted no short leash with all that adventure in front of me.

I'm still the same. So let's go ahead and get all of the *But . . . be sures* out of the way here. (Especially for those of you who aren't wired like me, and you can't relax and have any fun here until the boundaries are set.)

We just cannot approach a question as crucial and loaded as, "What am I supposed to do with my life?" without some sort of framework. Nearly every subject we discuss in this chapter will come up again in a deeper way, but let me lay it out for you here in general terms.

IS THIS ABOUT US OR GOD?

I read a book recently that I really appreciate; its message was to quit analyzing everything and just *do* something.[1] I couldn't agree more. As a culture, we are obsessed with analyzing ourselves and talking about ourselves, when at the end of the day, people are sick and dying. People don't know God. People are enslaved. People are going though divorces and depression and burying their children while we are figuring ourselves out!

I do believe, however, that for a very short—and I mean a *short*—season we can pull back and consider what specifically God may want from us here. As Zac and I were fumbling our way through seminary, we honestly did not know exactly why we were there. So we began the process of uncovering our unique place in God's plans. It felt like navel-gazing. I was nervous it was selfish, and I even resisted at first. As I was asking God for a peace about this season of self-discovery, Professor Howard Hendricks said these words in one of our classes: "You can't help anyone else until you understand yourself."

So this will not be self-analysis for the sake of inner fulfillment, though I believe deeper joy is a by-product. This is about understanding the story of God and how to play our parts in it, to serve him and his people while we are here.

When John Piper was asked how we find the will of God for our lives, he replied, "Know Scripture, know yourself, and know the need around you."[2] It is all right to go here, especially for the sake of God and others. Scripture supports this again and again:

GOD HAS PLACED THE PARTS IN THE BODY, EVERY ONE
OF THEM, JUST AS HE WANTED THEM TO BE. IF THEY
WERE ALL ONE PART, WHERE WOULD THE BODY BE?
AS IT IS, THERE ARE MANY PARTS, BUT ONE BODY.

1 CORINTHIANS 12:18-20

DO NOT NEGLECT THE GIFT YOU HAVE.

1 TIMOTHY 4:14 ESV

TO EACH IS GIVEN THE MANIFESTATION OF
THE SPIRIT FOR THE COMMON GOOD.

1 CORINTHIANS 12:7 ESV

There is a time and a place to search for our unique parts in God's story . . . *but* . . . here is my admonition:

Respond to the need you see. *Right now.*

"Give to everyone who asks you" (Luke 6:30). We are called to care for the things we see right in front of us, and anything else we can touch as well, regardless of our wiring and stories. As we live out our callings, we respond to need no matter what. Even today, as I write a book that fits directly into my calling, I am also overtipping the awesome Jamaican waiter serving me breakfast, who is sending money to his kids and wife back in Jamaica. With joy, he served me my meal. I even noticed a beautiful dignity that hinted he was living for something greater than just getting my order correct. And when I asked him about faith, he said that he loved Jesus.

So don't bother waiting around for a unique voice to come out of the sky. We move, respond, love, and obey. And as we go, God leads humble souls who are willing to be led.

To the question "Is it about us or about God?" I'd say, if *we* are about God, there's just no issue.

STAY OR GO?

I grew up certain that if I actually surrendered my life for God then he would most definitely send me to Africa. I thought nervously, *If there is need and I am willing, then why wouldn't he send me?* So because of fear and a most sincere, deep love of my close friends and Starbucks, I was thirty-plus before I finally said, "To heck with it. I'm in, whatever you say."

In my young mind, missionaries were likely the only fully surrendered superheroes of the faith. The rest of us were inclined toward comfort and materialism and an infatuation with the familiar. No, the truly godly sold all they owned and lived in huts somewhere. The next-highest level of superheroes committed to vocational ministry in the United States. Now, this thought makes me sick to write, because the most surrendered people I know are

- physicians in Austin, Texas, helping those who have battled depression their entire lives;
- that awesome Jamaican waiter who served me breakfast this morning and sends his check back home to his fourteen-year-old son and wife, and while he serves me, asks to see a picture of my family;
- our good friend Eric, who uses his gifts as an entrepreneur to start companies where every dime of the profit is funneled into orphan care;
- a stay-at-home mom who decided she could use her love for cooking and her home to have dinner parties, hosting over five hundred guests in her home in a year—just to bless them and connect them and build up their lives;
- our good friend Jon, who builds custom homes in Austin. As he lays bricks and kitchen counters with excellence, he also engages in deep relationships with his crew and each family he works for;
- my neighbor Corbin, who wanted to contribute a little extra income to her family, so she began a landscape company out of her home. When I see her, she always has dirt somewhere on her body, and she has never been happier. When you ask her why she is so happy, she says, "Because I am doing the thing that God put me on earth to do. I am making people's lives more beautiful."

However, some have prayed and given their lives, and they *were* called to go:

- Marty and Amy Skrivanos lived in Little Rock and had a comfortable life and income. But at forty, Marty sensed God's call to become a vocational counselor, after spending his entire life aware of this gift but unclear as to how to pursue it. In the middle of his life, with three kids, Marty left his career. They pulled their kids out of school, moved from extended family and financial security, and headed to Denver Seminary.

- Our good friends Gloria and Dave Furman knew they were going to leave a lot of family and comfort when they began the first evangelical English-speaking Christian church in downtown Dubai. They obeyed, and left every comfort of a familiar culture, and God is using them to impact one of the most influential parts of the world.

- Our other friends, Bill and Lisa Miller, knew they could take their love for God into Prague, but not as vocational ministers, so he is a professor at a local college. With his gifts and training, they have seen many people come to Christ there.

So do you stay or do you go? I do not know. I am not telling you to move. And I am not telling you to stay. Just to say, "God, have your way."

SMALL OR BIG?

I can't tell the difference between what the world thinks is big or small or what God thinks is big or small, because it is the wrong question, and I rarely ask it anymore.

The only question to ask here is:

"What am I supposed to do, God?"

And then do it. Don't analyze it; just do it. Like Joseph did. Joseph knew God deeply and trusted him. So much of his life was seemingly inconsequential, like scrubbing floors in Potiphar's house. But to him, scrubbing a floor with excellence mattered to God. Staring at a prison wall for years mattered because it was building the character of a man who would forgive the evil of his brothers, and who ultimately—and most importantly— would lead a country out of ruin.

At the end of our lives, when we stand before God, these are the only things that will matter.

In our culture, we judge with backward values and twisted motives. We love to make stars out of people and then watch them fall. We do this for sport. And then we crave that stardom that is so obviously not fulfilling. An old saying goes, "Do what you love and the money will follow." I don't know if you will love what God calls you to do (you might), and I certainly can't promise that money will follow (it may). But I can tell you that at the end of our lives, when we stand before God, these are the only things that will matter:

Did I do what God wanted me to be doing while I was here?

Did I complete the works he had for me?

Did I fulfill my purposes in my generation?

So instead of waiting until we're standing in God's throne room, let's work backward and ask those questions now. Let's live them today. Not for a salvation that can be earned, but in response to a God who built and rescued us as a part of his great purpose. If you are willing, he will lead you.

"Seek first his kingdom and his righteousness, and all these things will be given to you as well," Jesus said (Matt. 6:33). And Paul lived it: "I know what it is to be in need, and I know what it is to have plenty. I have learned the secret of being content in any and every situation" (Phil. 4:12). All that the world judged as important was inconsequential to Paul's mission, his God, and his soul. He explained: "But whatever gain I had, I counted as loss for the sake of Christ. Indeed, I count everything as loss because of the surpassing worth of knowing Christ Jesus my Lord" (Phil. 3:7–8 ESV).

So what is God calling you to do?

Will you start a nonprofit?

Will you start a Bible study in your office?

Will you pursue a career as an accountant?

Will you adopt a child?

Will you start an art program at your local school?

Will you run for office?

Will you start ministering in a nursing home?

Will you coach a Little League team?

Will you design homes?

Will you move to Africa?

Will you start a movement to end slavery?

Will you take care of your dad, who is ill?

Will you go on a short-term mission trip?

Will you write a book?

In response to my calling, some days I talk about Jesus in books, and some days in arenas, and some days in living rooms. And if I am across from my dear friend Christine Caine, one of the strongest runners I know, my obedience to God seems small. If I sit across from my dear friend Laura, who spends her days taking care of all the little people at her feet, she thinks my forms of obedience seem big. It is so relative.

Let's live from them today. Not for a salvation that can be earned, but in response to a God who built and rescued us as a part of his great purpose.

Comparison is often why our important roles shrink to seem so insignificant. Comparison robs us of the joy of obedience.

As I write to you, I've found myself in a number of coffee houses, beside a hospital bed, in a messy kitchen with something sticky on my elbows, in a little rented cabin in Gruene, Texas, and—blessed Almighty—today I write to you from a beach in Florida where I attended a conference earlier this week. Score.

But even the seemingly fun, meaningful jobs usually end up feeling mundane when your elbows are sticky from leftover breakfast milk.

The most inconspicuous tasks usually are building big things we can't see yet.

And a decade prior to all these new adventures, I changed diapers and scrubbed toilets and cooked chicken. I waded through a decade of the seemingly mundane, but if someone didn't change my children's diapers they would not be able to change the world. And you better believe a lot of my life is still full of it. Diapers and floors and food remind us that we are all human, and there is beauty and character formed in the mundane.

But the most inconspicuous tasks usually are building big things we can't see yet.

VOCATION OR CALLING?

Are we talking about our jobs or our callings here? In many ways, this is a similar question to "small or big?" And it has a similar answer.

For some of us, our careers are our callings, and we live out our callings while we are just doing a job. It is a rare gift to pay your bills as you fill up your soul. For most of the world and most every generation, work is about provision, not personal fulfillment. There is enough personal satisfaction in being able to feed your family.

Within the Western world, we have the luxury of millions of jobs in almost as many fields—even in times of economic crisis—and yet sometimes people complain about their unsatisfying jobs for years. Personally, I want to shake them and say, "We live in a world where you can change your job. Change it, for crying out loud!"

But sometimes we are called to stay in our places, even if it is the most mind-numbing, miserable thing in the world. We will talk more about this in part 3 when we start to journal. This is about something deeper than a job, yet we can't ignore our jobs. This is about how we spend our minutes and our days. Because eventually, our minutes and days equal our lives.

Eventually, our minutes and days equal our lives.

God calls people to all types of vocations. For example, David was a warrior and then a king. Nehemiah was a cupbearer and then a wall builder. Daniel and Joseph were counselors to national leaders, Jesus was a carpenter before a life in ministry, and Paul was a tentmaker. There are no such things as spiritual and secular jobs—we just made that up. God calls people to himself, and then to display him in every way, wherever we are. So are you called to teach or write or mother or build homes or fly planes? Beautiful. Do it as unto the Lord.[3]

God works—he builds and creates. God sees chaos and brings order, and his work is characterized by joy and service to us. You were made to create and build and reflect his image.

Work was given as a gift before the fall; we weren't made to sit around and do nothing. We were made to work in the mundane, but we aren't defined by the mundane. Because Jesus set us apart with a deep purpose to live out as we teach or write or mother or build homes or fly planes, there is no difference between a vocation and a calling. If you're showing God to the world in whatever job you're doing, you're on the right track.

WHAT WE CAN KNOW VS. WHAT WE CAN'T

My middle sister, Brooke, and her husband, Tony, run a guest ranch in Colorado called Lost Valley Ranch. They lead dozens of young staff, who beautifully host dozens of guests every week. On one of my recent visits to the ranch, the head chef, Matt, walked out of the kitchen to find me. We had never met, but I knew exactly who he was. He was coming to thank me. One insignificant and unknowing moment of my life had changed his, and he wanted to shake my hand.

Three years earlier, I sat in my car outside of Bible study with a young girl named Anne. She was twenty-two and finished with college, and as she watched her friends accepting jobs and making wedding plans, she felt lost. She wondered aloud what direction her life should take; the railroad tracks of the last twenty-two years had ended, and now she was forced to build her own track.

She was restless and uncertain, but she sat in my car holding on to a few things that only equaled confusion in her mind:

She loved to cook and she was good at it.

She had clear gifts of hospitality and leadership.

She wanted to use these things to minister.

As she talked, I wrote the name of the ranch and my sister's name and phone number down on a scrap of paper. She hopped out of the car, and the next thing I knew, my sister and her husband had hired her for the summer. The summer turned into three years, and waitressing turned into running the kitchen, and a cute chef turned into a fiancé named Matt.

The day I met Matt, we sat talking about God's brilliant planning. That night in my car, Anne didn't have even a hint of her future. But God had already written the story, and he placed that restless feeling in her that made her ask for a moment of my time.

He gave her enough knowledge of herself to lead her to a unique place, hundreds of miles from home, where he was writing another story that would eventually intersect with hers.

> No eye has seen,
>> no ear has heard,
> no mind has conceived
>> what God has prepared for those who love him.
>>>> (1 COR. 2:9)

God is accomplishing a thousand tiny purposes at any given moment around us. There is only so much we can know, but we can leave the stuff we can't know to God and believe he has it all worked out. It may feel quiet, and we possibly even feel forgotten, but God is moving to work out his plans all around us.

What is our part?

Trust.

CHAPTER 6

PLEASING GOD

Recently, I asked a string of questions on Facebook: "How do your motives hold you back from running headfirst into God's purposes for you? Should they hold us back? Or are we paralyzed by fear of ourselves?"

The conversation that exploded in the comment section of this post exposed that I wasn't the only one who was terrified of myself. AT&T has a marketing campaign rightly called "It's Not Complicated." A dorky guy in a suit asks little preschoolers questions like this:

"Which would you rather have: a big tree house or a small tree house?"

Then little kids rattle off their profound answers: "If it's big enough you can have a disco in your tree house." Awesome. And yes.

The takeaway is not complicated either: bigger, more, is always better.

But *bigger* and *more* is not always better. I have friends who live in bigger "tree houses," and they would be the first to tell you bigger tree houses cost a lot more time and money, the fancy disco balls break, and (contrary to what AT&T might have you think) more and bigger starts to get complicated quickly.

Ambition is complicated. *Bigger. More.* When related to material things it sounds like greed, so we often take the idea of "bigger and more" in our lives and boil it all down to sin. We sit in the back like my friend Jamie, who aches to dream, but says, "It always seems easier to sit on the back row and kill my dreams than to fight the sin that may be attached to those dreams."

We are afraid of big dreams because we are afraid of ourselves.

We are afraid of greatness because we are afraid of our arrogance.

And yet Jesus said of us, "Whoever believes in me . . . they will do even greater things than these" (John 14:12). It almost sounds blasphemous to do even greater things. We rarely say it, but when we start to have hints of great thoughts or visions, we often quickly dismiss them, afraid that we may be vain. Arrogant. Prideful. Or worse, simply that we would *appear* prideful.

I fight these wars in my soul nearly every day. For so long I just sat in the back, my dreams spilling out on the floor. But a few months ago I found myself in a room with a woman who did not seem to know how to dream small. She is a giant in the world of ministry, and we had the afternoon with her to ask any questions of her that we wanted. With a big vision growing in my heart, I knew exactly what I wanted to ask: "How do you know if a vision is from God?"

She looked down, and then very directly and simply said, "At some point you look at the motives of your heart, and if they are for God, then just do it."

It was simple and difficult all at the same time, because a convoluted mixture of motives undergirds every pursuit in life.

PARTS NO ONE SEES

As Zac and I prayed, "God, we will do anything," I knew the reason I had not been using my gifts in any great capacity was because I was afraid of appearing arrogant. When I was an eighteen-year-old, I knew I had the gift of teaching and I knew how to lead. For years I taught younger women in my living room. I looked around our community and saw so many women who needed more God. Though I knew I had visions of how to give him to them, I was paralyzed with this fear. Beginning a small Bible study in our church seems like no big deal now, but it was a painfully scary thought then.

I remember telling myself things like, *I will humbly sit in the back and give other people the chance to lead.* It sounds good. But I was completely disobeying God, and I wasn't playing the part in the body of Christ that God had designed me to play. Because by using my gifts, others would be released to use their gifts, and so on.

We need to quit apologizing for using our gifts and start apologizing for *not* using them. I would say to myself, *I am ministering to younger girls in my living room. That is enough. Greatness isn't in size.*

> We need to quit apologizing for using our gifts and start apologizing for not using them.

Of course it would have been enough, if God wasn't calling me to something more. Some people charge mountains with no fear of themselves, and they need to check their motives. Some never take a mountain because of too much fear of themselves, and checking those motives is just as important.

God exposed my false humility. Nervously, with the support of our church leaders, I offered my first public study, *Stuck*, to our small church plant. Somehow 150 women found their way to a little cafeteria, and I taught them how God designed the spaces within us to be full of only him. Christians' lives were turning upside down; some even wondered if they had ever truly been saved. Unbelievers found safety, and a dozen people received Christ in the months that followed. God had been wanting to move through me, and I had never let him because I was worried I would appear arrogant.

Near the end of the study, after watching God work in the most unbelievable ways, two people in the study voiced criticism about the very fears that had paralyzed me before: my motives. As I processed their criticism, I began to spin. Yes, the thing I most feared was happening. I had stepped out and led in our community, and I was potentially coming off as arrogant to people I cared about. I craved a return to the safety of the back row and the anonymity it once had given me.

As I shared the hurt from this with my friend Karen, rather than comfort me with all the good things that God had done, she simply asked me, "Is God pleased with you in this?"

Everything in me quit spinning, and with 100 percent certainty I answered, "Yes, he is."

I knew how difficult the last few months had been. In faith I had acted in obedience, pushing through my fears of approval to lead for his name's sake and for people's healing and freedom. I knew that God was pleased. I could not say that my motives were in the right place other times in my life, but this time I had complete peace.

Then Karen said, "Then what else is there?"

At the core of our souls lie our volitions, our wills, our deepest desires. Karen asked me a question she could not know the answer to. She asked me to reveal something that mere results and criticism or visible greatness or failure cannot reveal. She asked me if my motives were pure. She asked me if my heart was right before my God.

Every one of us was made to do great things, and it is why

something in us feels restless and discontent. Because deep down, we know we were created for some great purpose. And these great things we were built to do are for God, through God, and in God.

I know sometimes it feels impossible to sort out the heart. So let's do our best to pinpoint what could be going on in there.

TOWERS AND NAMES

Our fear of greatness originates in the right place, since we usually do struggle to have the right motives. Most of us would love to make a name for ourselves, and we spend a lot of our energy trying and trying, but at the same time trying not to look like we are trying.

When mankind was barely on the earth, God gave them one command: be fruitful and fill the earth (Gen. 1:28). His desire was that the whole earth would be full of his glory.

They were fruitful, but they kept it in one spot; they did not obey and fill the earth. They built cities and chose evil, and they tried their best to achieve personal greatness. So rather than doing something God had asked them to do, they thought of their own great idea. They wanted to build something in their strength. Rather than make God's name great for his glory, they sought to make a name for themselves for their own glory, and they built the tower of Babel.[1]

Little has changed since then. We were built for the greatness of God. But left to ourselves, we love being great more than we love making God great. So whether you are building the tower for your own name, or you are just too scared to even try to build anything because you don't want to look egotistical, both are wrong.

I have talked to enough of you to know that many of you are sitting on your gifts too. The enemy is subtle and warps truths into lies for us. He tells us we are being humble, responsible, and selfless, while we are killing the things God put us on the planet to do, the things that would build his kingdom.

Perhaps you have seen behind the facade of people doing great things in God's name, when in reality, they're just after the fame. We live in a world in love with fame. Almost anyone who works hard enough can find a way to get noticed and to make money doing so. Unfortunately, this is true as much in Christendom as it is anywhere. And while it is not our responsibility to judge anyone else's motives, it is very much our responsibility to scrutinize our own. And it's a good idea to do so daily. I know that while most days I drag my heels in following more public callings, when others start applauding me, all of a sudden I start waving and loving it. We all fight our divided motives every day. The key is to *fight*.

While it is not our responsibility to judge anyone else's motives, it is very much our responsibility to scrutinize our own.

So how do we fight? Whether you are building a name for yourself or sitting on the back row hiding so people won't judge you, the answer is the same: *we get over ourselves.*

OVER IT

Soon no name on this earth will matter but one. Not yours, not mine. That one name has asked you to build with him. And who wouldn't trade building sand castles to get to build something that lasts forever?

This makes me think of Moses when God appeared in a burning bush and told him, "I have seen the misery of my people in Egypt. I have heard them crying out, and I am concerned about their suffering. So *I* have come down to rescue them and to bring them up out of that land into a good and spacious land."[2]

Moses piped up with, "Who am I that I should go to Pharaoh and bring the Israelites out of Egypt?" (Ex. 3:11).

God had basically told him, "*I* see hurting people whom *I* want to set free." And all Moses could think was, *Me? You want me?* As if anything God was doing had a thing to do with him. God was going to do it all, for the sake of his people suffering in bondage. But Moses could not get over himself. Thankfully, God used him anyway.

Paul wrote, "If I were still trying to please men, I would not be a servant of Christ" (Gal. 1:10). Western mentality has shaped our views of work and success and calling so deeply that it is difficult to shake the idea of pleasing and impressing other people. God is asking us to get over it.

A GREAT SHIFT

We see big and small. We see secular and Christian. We see size and numbers. We decide what constitutes "important work." It feels impossible to sort out motives; it takes so much energy to go around with yardsticks, measuring and comparing and weighing everything.

Tim Keller defines meaningful work as taking the raw materials we are given and assembling them in a way that causes other people to flourish.[3] For instance, a gifted composer takes individual notes that alone just sound like noise, until she assembles them into something beautiful that causes others to flourish. An author takes words and does the same. An artist takes paint or clay or charcoal and does the same.

Now what about less creative, seemingly more mundane work? A housekeeper takes chaos and assembles order so that others will flourish in that environment. An accountant takes numbers and assembles them so that others can pay their taxes and flourish by avoiding prison. Mothers take the raw materials of their children and shape them into people who will one day help others flourish.

Good work. Hard work. Helping others. Those things have always been noble. Those things have always been respected. In Rwanda, where we adopted our son, when you talk to the men who work the fields, they speak as confidently and proudly of their contributions to this world as the attorneys in their suits.

But the game has changed for us. Somehow we have assembled different scales that weigh titles and incomes and even the amount of sacrifice a particular action requires. Some University of Texas sophomores recently told me over breakfast tacos that their friends all compete to do the most sacrificial things with their summers. Apparently it's as if you are sinful if you aren't going to a third-world country. We have hijacked the game, measuring worth with a scale that God did not create. Deciding whether to intern in a law office or head overseas for the summer isn't the issue; doing things for the applause of others is where we muddy our purposes.

After World War II, author Dorothy Sayers conducted a study on fulfillment. As she asked men about the most difficult days of their lives, when they watched friends die and fought for their own lives, nearly every one of them said they had never been more fulfilled.

Why?

A beautiful motivation emerged, and it wasn't about the appearance of the work. Personal fulfillment is fullest when we are involved in something bigger than ourselves, something for the good of others. While the college kids were looking for their own glory, the soldiers were involved in a master plan. Both groups were about noble work, but one was competing for praise and one was settled on the good of others.

What if we took the pieces of our lives (no matter what the

world says they are worth) and began to use them to help others flourish for the sake of Christ? All of a sudden our motives would narrow to contain more of God and others, and less of us.

Is it so wrong to want to make a big impact with your days here, for God?

EMBRACING THORNS

I used to watch people in the limelight of ministry with a little bit of jealousy. They seemed to be magically using their gifts and seemed so fulfilled—so happy. They appeared to be honoring God, and then as an added bonus, to possess all of our respect and admiration. *How rewarding*, I thought. Until . . . that light shined on me just a little.

I'm a pastor's wife and speaker and writer, and it is not fancy, easy, or ego stroking. So far it has felt like death—and not a clean, swift, bullet-through-the-heart kind of death. No, it's a slow, drawn-out, when-is-this-going-to-be-over thing.

Scrutiny and opinions have found us. Battling Satan . . . not really a highlight. And juggling the weight of leading people to God—while trying to pull off godly mom and wife and friend and carpool driver . . . heavy balls to toss around.

See, God has a means of shaping our motives. He wants our hearts to be pure. He is changing us, humbling us, making our hearts beat for him.

> To keep me from becoming conceited because of these surpassingly great revelations, I was given a thorn in my flesh, a messenger of Satan, to torment me. Three times I pleaded with the Lord to take it away from me. But he said to me, "My grace is sufficient for you, for my power is made perfect in weakness." (2 Cor. 12:7–9)

The things that make this calling weighty are the very things that keep my head down in it. Thorns push us to need God, and as I make my way through my thorns, I remember my humanity, my insecurity, my fear, my sin. I rustle through them all, knowing that through all this unbelief and fear and selfishness, he is on the other side. I wish it were easier. But then again, it would cost nothing and mean nothing if it were. And knowing me, I'd go looking for the limelight instead of for God.

I think in twenty years, we will regret more of the things we didn't do than things we did imperfectly.

What if we just ran through our thorns and our sin and let God straighten us out as we go? We can't wait until our sin is gone before we run, or we never will. We have to fight it *as* we run. I think in twenty years, we will regret more of the things we didn't do than the things we did imperfectly.

Recently, I listened as Larry King interviewed Daniel Radcliffe about the final *Harry Potter* movie, and Daniel said a beautiful thing about his role in these epic films: "I always knew that anyone who was given this role would have the same fame. It was never about me. It was about this franchise. I was simply a part of something bigger."[4]

We have all been given roles in a story that is about something so much bigger; it just isn't about us. After all that living on the back row, afraid of stealing God's glory, a reality check is in order. Who am I to even think such a thing? As my friend Christine Caine says, "Who am I to dare think, that on my very best day, I could ever take one little piece of the glory of God?"

So we throw off the sin that entangles and we run . . . But where do we run?

CHAPTER 7

A PARABLE

When I met Christ, he set me on a track, and I began running a race with fervor, surrounded by people cheering. I felt motivated, purposeful, full of joy. My eyes weren't distracted. Jesus was in full focus, and the point of this race felt clear. But as I ran, I noticed more and more people tangled up in the weeds, to my left and right. Some of them had stopped running, distracted by something, and some of them had stopped because they were in pain.

I kept running, but I began to feel lonely. So I began to ask myself questions that were once clear to me: *Why am I running again?*

Then I tripped. I was hurt.

Now I was the one on the side of the road. I was tired and in pain. It felt good to stop running. I pulled myself close to some other hurt runners. We told stories and jokes, and eventually we were comfortable together. As if there weren't even a race—as if we weren't even hurt.

Every once in a while a runner called to me, "Come on, Jennie! Come back and run with us!" But no one ever stopped to really help me. They just ran by. As time passed, I picked up some entertaining hobbies on the side of the road. The hobbies temporarily motivated me and made me feel a little fulfilled again. My injured ankle never fully healed, but I quit thinking about it—it did not hurt quite as badly as it used to. And before long, we discovered great entertainment in critiquing the remaining runners—their shorts, hair, pace, attitude.

Until one day a small pack of runners turned off the road and headed toward me. I wished they would go away. But they didn't. I remembered passing them back when I was running; they had been on the side of the road with injuries, all tangled up. They ran right up to me and sat down.

One of them handed me water and another one had medical supplies. They asked me a question:

"Do you need help?"

For some reason I said yes, and before I finished uttering the word they were wrapping my ankle, giving me food and water, and talking to me about the race again—about how much I had missed, how much they needed me. "We want you to run the rest of the way with us. It is really getting exciting, and we don't have much farther."

Something dead inside me woke up. A fire relit itself in my chest. My ankle still hurt, but I didn't care. I just wanted to recklessly run with all my heart again, because they reminded me of the reason that we run.

I am running to bring glory to my Father God, who gave me a purpose and a hope when I was unworthy, on the side of the road, broken. Now our little misfit team stops for every runner we see on the side of the road. We stop and offer them the same healing and hope that was offered to us. I sense God's pleasure as we run and as we stop for those who have fallen off to the side.

Something in me physically craves the last part of that story. I crave freedom to run. "It is for freedom that Christ has set us free. Stand firm, then, and do not let yourselves be burdened again by a yoke of slavery" (Gal. 5:1). You were running a good race. Who cut in on you? Where did you get off track?

FOUR STARTING PLACES

We all come into this search for greater purpose from different places, and all of us will need different things through this process. This road will be unique to every person who goes through this experience. It is important to recognize where you are in our race.

Numb

Maybe you are on the side of the road, or maybe you are still in the race. You don't know if you are living on purpose or not. You are busy and surviving and somewhat content. Maybe sometimes you are bored, but in general your life is full and you aren't one to overanalyze. Maybe you are beginning to wake up and hurt for more, but even that sentence just made you nervous.

QUESTIONS YOU MAY BE ASKING

"Shouldn't I just feel thankful for what I have instead of wanting more?"

"What is wrong with being comfortable and happy?"

"Isn't it enough just to be faithful where I am?"

To you, I would say this: "There is a time for everything. . . . A time to search and a time to give up . . . a time to tear and a time to mend, a time to be silent and a time to speak," and on and on (Eccl. 3:1, 6–7).

This may be your time to tear up and your time to search and speak and consider. For a short season, I want you to consider that there may be more. Because I would rather you be unsettled for a minute, and sure that you are in the will of God, than content in the wrong place.

Thirsty

You are on the side of the road, and you are ready for someone to come show you the way back into the race. You hurt. Inside you are longing for more. You are begging for clearer purpose than you currently feel. But you don't know if your restless heart is your enemy making you unsettled, or your friend pushing you toward greater things. You are not satisfied, but you don't know what to do about it. You are asking yourself, "Is there more? And if there is, how do I find it?"

QUESTIONS YOU MAY BE ASKING

"Is it wrong to want more?"

"Does God have some secret purpose that I am missing?"

"What if there is no clear direction? What then?"

The apostle Paul wrote from prison, "I urge you to live a life worthy of the calling you have received" (Eph. 4:1).

There remained a restlessness in Paul throughout his life. He urgently went about the work of God and asked us to do the same. I don't know if your restless heart is sinful or from God. But I do know that God often awakens and moves me toward more with a deep discontentment and an unsettling feeling of dissatisfaction. Many times when I longed for more, sure enough, he had more for me. We will deal with all of these questions, so don't preach away that restlessness yet.

Running Free

Some of you are living it. You feel purpose. You are running hard after God and are being obedient, and you have watched God move around you. You know what you are made to do, and perhaps you are already doing it. You have already moved through a season of feeling numb or satisfied and you've become restless and found more. Life is full and hard, but rich and fulfilling too.

QUESTIONS YOU MAY BE ASKING

"Do I even need this?"
"I already know the answers to a lot of these questions, so why should I keep reading?"

"Let us throw off everything that hinders and the sin that so easily entangles. And let us run with perseverance the race marked out for us, fixing our eyes on Jesus, the pioneer and perfecter of faith . . . so that you will not grow weary and lose heart" (Heb. 12:1–3).

Some of my friends who are running the hardest have said they need this project more than anyone else, because we all forget. I have been in all three places over and over again, and you will too. We start running the race we were meant to run, and then we realize after mile five that we have accidentally signed up for a marathon. And before we know it, we are bored or restless all over again. I pray these words would hand you water on your run. Let them fill you with new strength and focus. Let them remind you afresh of your calling so that you will keep running and not grow weary. We are not home yet, and I pray that this study will help you persevere in your race.

> *We start running the race we were meant to run, and then we realize after mile five that we have accidentally signed up for a marathon.*

At the Starting Line

Or maybe you've realized that you don't really know God, that you don't actually have a personal relationship with him, where you talk every day and you look to him and live for him. If that's the case, then before you go any further, read the "How to Find God" page in the back of this book. It'll be the best, most important thing you'll ever do.

We are about to begin the process of identifying the unique threads God has given you, but before we begin it is important you know where you start this process.

PART 2

THE
THREADS

CHAPTER 8

THE PROCESS

Zac was doing more and more ministry and God was blessing it, but as we were finishing seminary he was still waiting for a magical moment. The moment when all the clouds part and God's voice booms from heaven, "Zac Allen, you are officially called into ministry."

I painfully watched and prayed as he struggled to find what it was he was made to do. Zac grew up in west Texas, in Abilene, the son of the high school football coach in a land where only two things exist: God and football. For many, the two words are actually synonymous. From a young age, he knew he would follow his father and become a football coach. However, as he neared college graduation and expected to take a position on his father's staff, one of the school's bylaws stating that children cannot be employed by their parents interrupted his plans.

I imagined he would quickly find another position in a small Texas town, but he seemed hesitant. As we plotted and prayed, Zac said one night, "I find myself thinking more about the ministry I could have through football than football itself."

He had watched hundreds of napkins fill up with Xs and Os across the dinner table as his dad worked out plays for the next day's practice. And while he adored his dad, his own brain didn't fantasize about football plays, and he wasn't sure he wanted it to.

So after a couple random jobs in business, he slowly, insecurely, and uncertainly began a life in vocational ministry. After a few years, seminary felt like the right next step. But as he stared at his future, he still wanted confirmation that this was where he was called to be.

We were just taking the next steps, and these seemed to be the steps God was laying in front of us. We were willing and somewhat able, and God was giving us what we needed to do the work of ministry, but we were so unsure of ourselves. We were hurting for a better understanding of ourselves and where we could most contribute in life. We were asking the question many of you are asking: *What do you want from us, God?*

We were also twenty-five. A rarely discussed secret is that almost all of us flail through our twenties. And one big reason is that we don't know ourselves yet.

We are just barely learning

- what we are good at;
- what we are terrible at;
- how our stories could ever be helpful to others;
- how to follow the Holy Spirit;
- how to not be a selfish brat;
- how to really love;
- what our passions are.

But to be perfectly fair, I meet people all the time who are fifty-plus and still trying to figure it out.

I was reasonably clear about my gifts back then, but I was terrified to use them. I held my passions and burdens close to my chest. At times it felt as if my chest would explode with it all contained, but I was paralyzed by what it meant for a woman to lead in ministry. Growing up in the conservative South, I had very few role models who were confidently using gifts similar to mine in vocational ministry. In a year I would graduate as a young wife and mother, holding gifts, training, a clear calling from God, and three babies. What was I supposed to do with it all?

I remember Zac glancing over with slight envy at my clarity and passion, as I glanced over with slight envy at the seeming freedom and potential his gender brought. We were doing our best to support each other, but we were also neck-deep in confusion about our places and purposes on this earth.

So in this foggy season of our lives, a mentor—someone very in touch with our flailing—pulled us aside and recommended we attend an intense process that our seminary built called LEAD. LEAD exists to clarify callings for leaders in ministry. It was a very expensive and time-intensive commitment, but it seemed to promise the thing we most needed: direction. So we did what many broke twentysomethings do when they can't afford something: we called and begged our parents and grandparents for the money.

Thanks to their generosity, we headed into a week of intense analysis and counseling to discover what we were supposed to do with our lives.

If that week hadn't changed our lives, I can say, I would not be writing this book. Some of what we discovered there was so crucial to our discipleship that it convinced me that a similar process is necessary for all believers.

Fears were beaten back, gifts and callings were clarified, and direction was narrowed.

As I mentioned earlier, Tim Keller says that as humans we all hold different raw materials. And the purpose of life's work is to work our raw materials into something excellent for the betterment of mankind.[1] We have to first understand what raw materials we have been given. These materials—what I've referred to before as threads—are given to us by God and for God. And we were built to run wild with them, so it is a valuable process to uncover and untangle them.

This idea can also be put into a simple equation (I should mention, I am anything but formulaic, but I want to give you a clear understanding of where we are headed):

God's Story + my threads + the need + the Holy Spirit = my purpose.

And the unabridged version of the equation:

The story of God through Scripture + an understanding of myself and my resources + taking inventory of the need around me + the mystery of following the Holy Spirit's leading = obediently living our purposes. (Perhaps—no promises.)

WHAT DO YOU HOLD?

My hope is that you will build a working understanding of the ways you have been created, the stories that have been given to you, the passions in your soul, the people in your path, the places you are to be, and the purposes the Holy Spirit is calling you toward.

When Jesus was about to do one of the most notable and beautiful miracles of his life here, he looked around and saw that thousands of people around him were hungry. Then, rather than create something out of nothing (which he was obviously capable of) he said to his disciples essentially, "Does anyone have any food?"[2]

One of the disciples found a little boy with a few fish and loaves of bread. Then Jesus fed thousands with the few materials that the little boy held. That little boy had something of value in his hands: it was a starting place. It was the something that great things could be birthed from.

It was a starting place. It was the something that great things could be birthed from.

We hold things. We don't think much about it, but there are hungry people all around us, and God is looking to take the seemingly insignificant little pieces tucked away in our lives to multiply them and feed his people.

This journey is a chance to lay out what you have, what you know, and hand it up to God. I should mention: we have no idea what he will say to do with it, but we begin by laying it out and handing it over.

WHY DOES IT MATTER?

As we discussed earlier, we want to live our lives intentionally. Without some effort, we will waste our minutes, our days . . . our lives. So putting thought into intentionally spending our time and resources for the glory of God may be the most important thing we will do with our lives.

As we understand ourselves in light of God's purposes, we are

- moved to action;
- able to filter opportunities as they present themselves;
- equipped with a compass pointing toward God's purposes for our lives;
- convicted that we are a part of a bigger story.

WHAT DO YOU NEED?

Prayer

Ask God to lead this process for you, to bring to mind memories, and to give supernatural insight and discernment as you process these important subjects.

People Who Know You

Gather together a few friends or family members who know you. Family can help you process and remember memories in your past. They can also remind you of what you were great at as a kid. Also, you need friends who can speak truth into this process, and hold you accountable as you move in faith in some of these directions. Gather them and ask them if you can do this together.

Reflection

As I said earlier, you are about to interact. So if you are reading this on your Kindle, get a journal and a pen. Likely, even if you are reading a paperback you will need more space to process than we could provide for you here. You should not read this without responding in written form somewhere.

All these things will help you get moving and support you as you deal with the fear that inevitably comes from stepping out like this. Remember, "Twenty years from now you will be more disappointed by the things that you didn't do than by the ones you did do . . . Sail away from the safe harbor. Catch the trade winds in your sails. Explore. Dream. Discover."[3]

No greater question sits deep in our souls as humans than . . . "Why am I here?"

But most of us can't answer it with any conviction for ourselves, even those of us who know God. Perhaps we could take a stab at why humans are here—but *why did God take the time to craft my days and life?* That one gets tricky. We hope we aren't accidents, and we try to believe that God has brilliantly diverse and specific purposes for our short lives here. But we don't know what they are, and deep down I think most of us doubt.

Let's tackle that weighty question. But before we do, take some time and process where you find yourself today in this journey.

LOOKING BACK

JOURNAL

Looking back at some of the things you have already processed
from part 1, answer the questions below in the space provided
or in your personal journal.

When you anticipate dreaming, what are you afraid of?

Do you feel discontent right now? How does that
discontentment tie into a desire for purpose?

Have your motives ever stopped you from doing something you
wanted to do for God? What were those dreams?

What do you most hope to get out of this process?

CHAPTER 9

THE PROJECT

I've heard it said that we will be the first entire generation to have a public record of our lives. Because of Instagram, Facebook, blogs, Twitter, and e-mails, our great-grandchildren will likely be able to Google the sum of our lives. When most of us Google our great-grandfathers now, we are lucky if an obituary shows up.

The story of our lives is adding up. What story will we tell? Of course, pictures and tweets could never tell the real story. The most sacred moments of our lives are bottled inside us—the moments that flash in your mind when your soul had never been so satisfied, or the moments you wish you could forget because you have never felt so much pain. *These* are the actual stories of our lives. That sounded a little like the opening to *Days of Our Lives*—but you get it. Most of these moments go unreported and unanalyzed.

TANGLED UP

For the last several months, a room full of women in Austin, Texas, have been working through this material together to identify the threads that make up their purposes. We've dug into the life of Joseph in Genesis. As you know, for a lot of us, this study fell in the midst of watching our best friend, Sarah, nearly die. But she made it, and now she has to begin the long journey of relearning to walk and talk. So we approached Scripture and big questions about God's purposes with a lot of tears. Joseph has become a bit of a fellow sojourner beside us through this dark season.

From an early age, Joseph had dreams and revelations from God. He specifically dreamed that his brothers and parents would all bow down to him one day. Joseph's ten older brothers hated him for this, and they sold him into slavery, allowing their father to believe he was killed. Joseph lived dark years as a slave in the house of Potiphar, but he served diligently. Nevertheless, Potiphar's wife lied and accused him of rape. He was imprisoned for more than a decade. Joseph spent more than twenty years either enslaved or in prison in Egypt.

But the dream Joseph dreamed as a child would come to fruition. He used his gift of dream interpretation and went on to help Pharaoh lead Egypt out of a great famine. He was given tremendous authority, second only to Pharaoh himself. What his brothers and others had meant for evil, God meant for good and for the saving of many lives. There is so much we can draw from Joseph's story. Like him, you've been given gifts, and you've been dealt a hand in life that may look incomprehensible. But we can also come closer to understanding these gifts and how they play into God's plans.

We've watched Joseph be so sure of God and his gifts—perhaps a little arrogant about it—and then we watched him face rejection and betrayal from his older brothers, who were supposed to protect him and never leave him. We've watched him serve his guts out as a slave, only to be falsely accused when he was doing the right thing. We've watched him sit in a prison cell for over a decade as he continued to talk about God and trust him.

When we've wanted to be so mad at God, we have been stopped by this man who trusted him through suffering, even though God was making no sense.

Joseph was full of a hope that disarmed the very worst kinds of loneliness and suffering. He was filled with a purpose that transcended his seemingly purposeless circumstances. And then at the end of a twenty-year tunnel of suffering and isolation, a light broke through in glaring form. Finally, he got to see what all of the difficulty was for. To those of us who could not see the light of relief and purpose yet—and perhaps won't this side of heaven—we tasted something bigger than pain and circumstance.

God was not far or flippant; he was strategically executing the most brilliant of plans to save lives. Joseph lifted our heads here in Austin to remind us that wheelchairs, words unspoken, three young kids who are missing their mama's kisses, parents in their seventies nursing their thirty-five-year-old daughter, and a divorce continuing to unfold while Sarah lies in a hospital bed—are not invisible to him. He knows, and he will take this hell on earth and someday show us how hell was building heaven.

My favorite thing about the way God communicates to us is that through his word, God often *shows* it to us gently, like in Al-Anon. It's like we're sitting in folding chairs with a circle of broken people who testify to a sovereign God who is loving, good, and perfect in his will—even if it looks like chaos. So we will bring the messy threads that make us human to him and see if he will sort them out.

In Austin, I can tell you—our band of sisters, we are not the same since we started doing this. We have tasted freedom and focus. I began our group in Austin with this massive disclaimer: "I do not know if this project will work, but will you just try this with me?"

God could untangle your soul, your story, your gifts, your people, your place, and your passions, and begin to weave it into purposes that you haven't been brave enough to imagine.

Now I've seen it work in many of the people I do life with. They were restless, searching, a little numb, bored, and very unsure with me that this little project could be any part of healing. But we changed—we were set a little more free and saw our paths a lot more clearly.

So I need to say this . . .

I think God could untangle your soul, your story, your gifts, your people, your place, and your passions, and begin to weave it into purposes that you haven't been brave enough to imagine.

DIFFICULT STUFF

We are about to transcend the realm of comfortable reading. This is going to get into your business. Even if you and I were sitting across from each other having coffee and figuring this out (which I deeply wish could be the case), a supernatural breakthrough would need to occur. Tackling the specific and intricate pieces of your life will take God plopping himself in the middle of us and issuing discernment and revelation through black-and-white words on a page and many notes marked in a journal. This is a process. But like my friends and I did, you will come out of this different. You may even glimpse God and his grand design for your threads.

I don't know if you are sitting in a bed about to nod off or if you are on an airplane or beach or in a coffee shop or surrounded by little toddlers pulling on you. All journeys have a cost. The path to our purpose here is rarely built comfortably. So are you restless enough to go here? Are you hungry enough for more to do the work?

I read no more than three-fourths of nearly every book I pick up. I am arrogant like that—once I figure out what the author is saying, I set it down. If you're like that, too, from this point on in the book, commit to finish. Here's why: it wasn't until the last two weeks of this process that we started to see what God was weaving with our lives. So even if there are parts of this journey you do not understand, keep going.

Ugh! I wish I wish *I wish* I could sit across from each one of you and look in your eyes and look at all you will write down—all the beautifully unique threads God has given you. I would cry with you when you shared the very worst moments of your life, and I would probably laugh at how ridiculously unsure you are of your gifts that are *so* obvious to everyone who knows you. We would pray about your place in God's story, and we would dream together, and point each other back to Scripture again and again to remind us that this is all real and worth it.

I know I would like you, and if you shared all of that with me—I would love you. I am sorry I can't hold your hand through this with more than words. But will you feel me with you through these words? I am crying as I type them, picturing you about to embark on this brave journey. And I am with you, cheering and praying and begging God to move for you as he has for me and for my friends.

My peace is that God is with you carrying on the good work he began in you, and oh, I pray these next few chapters will be just that. God revealing and speaking and moving you deeper into his love for you and his plans for you.

Praise be to the God and Father of our Lord Jesus Christ, the Father of compassion and the God of all comfort, who comforts us in all our troubles, so that we can comfort those in any trouble with the comfort we ourselves receive from God. (2 Cor. 1:3–4)

He is with you, loving you and comforting you and leading you so that we can love and comfort and lead others to him.

JOSEPH'S STORY

Before we begin, it would be helpful to read through Joseph's story, found in Genesis 37–50. Here is a chart of some of the major events of Joseph's life.

SOLD INTO
SLAVERY
BY HIS
BROTHERS

PROSPERS
IN
POTIPHAR'S
HOUSE

GOD GIVES
JOSEPH VISION
THAT HE
WILL RULE

THROWN
INTO
PRISON
IN EGYPT

MADE
RULER
IN EGYPT

JOURNAL

From the scriptures and story of Joseph:

Describe the journey to Joseph's purpose.

Describe Joseph's attitude throughout his journey.

How might he have felt in the decades of suffering?

What do you think God's perspective on Joseph's sufferings was?

CHAPTER 10

THE IMMOVABLE FABRIC

My son Cooper was born and lived three and a half years of his life in Africa. He is five now and is wrestling with the fact that his skin color is a few—strike that—a *lot* of shades darker than his brother's and mine and Zac's and his sisters'. He keeps running his hand up and down my arm and asking me, "Where can we go that I can get skin like this?" My insides fall apart.

He doesn't know the painful history of his skin color in our country yet. Right now he just wants to be like his family. His identity is unique in our family. He has a heritage that each of us appreciates deeply, but we do not share. So he quietly asks me as we lie in bed before prayers:

"Why did God make me born in Africa?"

"Why did God put me in another mommy's tummy?"

"Why did God make me?"

I can't deny that the answers to many of my son's questions are painful. Abandonment usually undergirds the beautiful tragedy of adoption, and finding himself in a loving family now can never make that painful truth go away.

It's usually dark as we lie in bed to pray and talk, and Cooper doesn't know that every time he asks me these questions I have tears running down my face as I preach my guts out in his bottom bunk. And ya'll better believe I turn all charismatic preacher. Because I want nothing more than for Cooper to believe what I am about to say to him.

"Not one part of you is by accident. God made you and placed you in your African mama's tummy, but he knew even then that I would be your forever mama and we would be your forever family. We were made for you and you were made for us.

"Cooper, you were made to show the world God, so God gave you a special story because he has a very special purpose for you while you are here. Everything God gives you, your Africa, your America, your dark skin and your strong legs, your hurts, your words, your blessings, your smart mind . . . everything you have is to use for God while you are here.

"And God will show you how. Soon we will be in heaven with God forever, and while we are here now, we get to use all we have to love people for God."

My five-year-old needs to know his life was on purpose and for a purpose. He wants to know he wasn't an accident. I can't take away the pain of his story, but I can tell him there is purpose. We all want to know we are not accidents. We all want to know our stories are going somewhere on purpose.

We are all built with something deep down in us to live for a story bigger than ourselves—the story of the one who made us. "He has . . . set eternity in the hearts of men" (Eccl. 3:11).

But Cooper will never make sense of his life until he understands that eternal story and the one who made him and placed him in his spot. It's a big earth, and when he studies it, he sees countries separated by a huge ocean, and he feels lost and small in it.

I think a lot of us feel lost and small.

That's part of the reason we so desperately want to find "God's will for me." We want to know that we exist on purpose and for a purpose. But we only ever discover God's will for us within God's will for this earth, for eternity, and for his people.

Why are we here? "For in him we live and move and have our being" (Acts 17:28).

GOD'S STORY OF HIMSELF

"Let us make mankind in our image, in our likeness, so that they may rule over the fish in the sea and the birds in the sky, over the livestock and all the wild animals, and over all the creatures that move along the ground."[1]

So I created mankind in our own image, in the image of God, I created them; male and female I created them.[2]

You exist on purpose and for a purpose. I built you and set you on this earth as a display of my love and my image.

But I have an enemy.

And my enemy came for you. He placed doubt in you—doubt that I am God and doubt that I am good and doubt that I love you. And you listened, and you chose death instead of me.

But before the creation of the world I made a plan. I actually chose you for me before you ever were born, before this whole story started. I picked you to be holy and blameless in my sight. But there wasn't one of you on earth who did what was right and never sinned.[3]

So I made a plan to get you back.

I planted a seed, and it grew throughout all of history. First Abraham, then Moses, then David. I would whisper of my plans through prophets and priests, like the prophet Hosea, whom I asked to marry a prostitute. I needed you to see, not just hear of, my love and pursuit of you. I wanted you to know that our relationship could not be thwarted by your sin; I would commit to you despite your sin. In the fullness of time, the fruit of that seed would destroy our enemy—he would crush the enemy's head and purchase my children, his brothers and sisters, back for me.

Long before I laid down earth's foundations, I had you in mind. I had settled on you to be made whole and holy by my love. Long, long ago, I decided to adopt you into my family through Jesus Christ. In my pleasure and will, I would freely give you the right to become the children of God.[4] I make stars and universes, and everything in them is my possession, but it was still my pleasure to adopt you as my child. You would become brothers and sisters to my beloved Son, the one who would die for your sin.

There was a ransom to be paid. Only a perfect lamb could buy the debt for the sum of your sin.

So for a joy that was set before him, my Son, Jesus, paid the ransom with his blood. He bled out to buy you back.

And these are only outskirts of my ways; how small a whisper of me—no eye has seen nor mind imagined what is in store for you.[5]

I know you are discontent here because you weren't made to live in this temporary, broken place. For a little while you are in this tent, groaning and burdened. But soon what is mortal will be swallowed up by life. I made you for this very purpose and have given you my Spirit as a deposit, a guarantee of what is to come.[6] My Spirit is me with you. I will not leave you. I will equip you for every good work I have planned for you here.[7] I will comfort you as you wait. I will remind you this is all real.

To help you persevere so that when you have accomplished my will here, you will receive what I have promised.

"Yet a little while,
and the coming one will come and will not delay."[8]

For your accuser, who accuses you before me day and night, has been hurled down.[9]

You will triumph over him by the blood of the Lamb and by the word of your testimony; and because you did not love your lives so much as to shrink from death.[10]

I am on my way; my "steadfast love endures forever" and ever.[11] In a little while I am coming and I will take you to the place I am.[12]

—God

God's story is our story too. C. S. Lewis described the lion Aslan (Jesus) in a beautiful way:

And as He spoke, He no longer looked to them like a lion; but the things that began to happen after that were so great and beautiful that I cannot write them. And for us this is the end of all the stories, and we can most truly say that they all lived happily ever after. But for them it was only the beginning of the real story. All their life in this world and all their adventures in Narnia had only been the cover and the title page: now at last they were beginning Chapter One of the Great Story which no one on earth has read: which goes on forever: in which every chapter is better than the one before.[13]

BUILT FOR GLORY

A line stretches out as far as the mind can imagine, with no end in sight. This is the unending story of our God, who ran after us to make us his children. Our pixel of a life, one dot of his eternal arrow.

My little Cooper, and Rahab and Oprah and Abraham Lincoln and Alexander the Great, and every other single human on the face of the earth, have found their stories in the confines of God's story. The history of the world fits in a small crevice of the history of God. And throughout that history, God is after one great purpose.

To understand our purposes, we must understand God's ultimate agenda.

God is most after his glory. And glory is the visible expression of God's goodness and beauty on this earth. It's how we recognize him.

The ultimate visible expression of God's glory on earth is Jesus. How did he live out the reflection of his Father here? "For I have come down from heaven not to do my will but to do the will of him who sent me" (John 6:38). Jesus followed God's will for him.

Concerning the story of God, we have a tremendous responsibility. We are to live out the same call. God has chosen to show himself and his goodness—his glory—through us. And like the millions of pixels that together are displaying *Duck Dynasty* on my TV right now as my kids are watching in the other room, every one of our unique callings will display God to our world. When we finally got a flat-screen TV, my husband set it up only to discover that one of the tens of thousands of pixels was out. One dumb pixel just didn't show up, and the entire display was affected. That TV went back.

Believe me, I know it feels near ridiculous to live for things we can't see yet. At the base of our souls we need to figure out whether we are building God's glory or our own. This could be the biggest hurdle we must cross before living our purposes. No matter how magnificent your pixel here, remember we will only ever be one brief little light unless we are part of the bigger thing we were made for.

> Just as a body, though one, has many parts, but all its many parts form one body, so it is with Christ. . . .
>
> Now if the foot should say, "Because I am not a hand, I do not belong to the body," it would not for that reason stop being part of the body. . . .
>
> The eye cannot say to the hand, "I don't need you!" And the head cannot say to the feet, "I don't need you!". . . So that there should be no division in the body, but that its parts should have equal concern for each other.
>
> Now you are the body of Christ, and each one of you is a part of it. (1 Cor. 12:12–27)

He built us uniquely, issuing different gifts and stories and places and people, then calls us to move as *one*. So whether our role is to mother or start a business or sponsor a child or sweep a floor or run a bank or teach little people to read, we don't want to miss it.

His Spirit will pour us into need, and who are we to judge where and what is the greatest need? This isn't as much about what or where; this is about getting over ourselves and just doing it.

But dadgumit, I am selfish. And so are you. We won't do this perfectly. God overcomes us and our distracted rebel selves with: Christ. "He is the radiance of the glory of God and the exact imprint of his nature, and he upholds the universe by the word of his power. After making purification for sins, he sat down at the right hand of the Majesty on high" (Heb. 1:3 esv).

Christ in us is our hope for a world we can't see yet. For the joy set before him, he endured the cross. It is a joy that we share: his joy was us, and our joy is him. It means forever with a God who is entirely good, and who chose us in him to become his children.

I want to have a faith God can move through.

SECURE

The rudder that keeps us fixed is our identity in Christ. We leave behind a life spent proving ourselves when we find the freedom of covering our mistakes and our inadequacy with the holiness and power of our Savior. We get to run with confidence, not in ourselves but in our God.

I want Cooper to understand he isn't just made for *a* purpose; he was placed in this time and space for the *greatest imaginable* purpose. He will show God to a world that doesn't know him—in his beautiful and unique way. He will bring light to darkness. He will assemble the pieces of his life, not into a tower for his own name that would only crumble, but for the name of the one God Almighty.

Well, he's five, and currently we are working on not throwing rocks, but that's the hope—that's my prayer—that's the sermon he's going to keep hearing.

"Faith is confidence in what we hope for and assurance about what we do not see" (Heb. 11:1).

I'll be honest: I have given my life to this story, and there are still days I wonder if it is all real. It's okay if you waver sometimes. God holds us in place with him; we don't hold ourselves. Where your faith is weak, pray and ask him for more. My prayer is this:

Help our unbelief, God. Give us faith that your arrow never ends, and that to live as a part of it is the reason we were created. We get to be part of the story of God, and I want nothing more than to run with you, a God who would die for me.

We get to be part of giving people God. That's cool.

GOD'S STORY

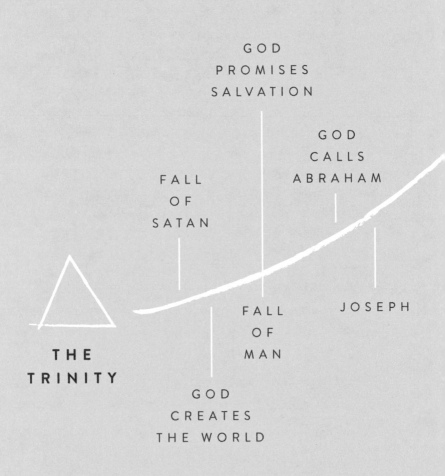

GOD
PROMISES
SALVATION

GOD
CALLS
ABRAHAM

FALL
OF
SATAN

JOSEPH

FALL
OF
MAN

**THE
TRINITY**

GOD
CREATES
THE WORLD

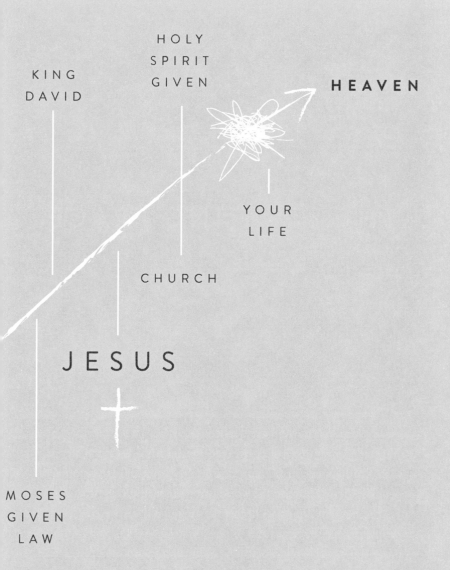

KING
DAVID

HOLY
SPIRIT
GIVEN

HEAVEN

YOUR
LIFE

CHURCH

JESUS

MOSES
GIVEN
LAW

JOURNAL

As you lift up above the everyday, what themes do you see?

What do you believe God's primary desires are for this story?

When you look at your life within this bigger story, what are your hopes for your place in it?

CHAPTER 11

THE STARTING PLACE

One night, as we wrestled through our stories together in our Austin class, Margaret leaned in to describe her passions. She adjusted her spunky, dark-rimmed glasses and described her job that also happens to be her passion. Margaret tells the stories of people suffering around the world using the medium of film. When I asked her why she loves her work, she quickly answered, "I want people to really be heard and understood. To be seen. And I want to move those watching to be a part of healing their hurt."

She doubted that these passions were in any way connected to her own story. So we asked her to tell us her story.

She showed little emotion as she described a childhood built in a home with no parents. She was the oldest of three siblings, and their dad had abandoned their family when they were very young. Their mom was not healthy and would leave them home alone while she went to unknown places for months at a time. Their grandparents lived next door and helped some, but Margaret carried the burden of caring for her little brother and sister.

We were all speechless, and tears flowed as we tried to imagine a home with no parents and three children turning the lights out and locking the doors and tucking themselves in at night.

But Margaret didn't cry and issued this disclaimer: "It's not a big deal. We were okay. We always had what we needed."

I whispered the only words that I could think. "Margaret— that is not okay. I am so sorry." Then she started to cry. She had learned to be brave, not complain, work hard. If she cried, who would have comforted her anyway? We did our best to allow her tears to fall in a safe space.

Then one of Margaret's close friends said, "Can you really not see that your story has birthed your passions?"

She still shook her head no, and we all shook our heads in disbelief that what screamed to us was invisible to her.

"You spend your life helping invisible people to be seen. To be heard. And you move others to respond to their need." She leaned back in her chair, uncomfortable with the thought but allowing it to press in.

What if the darkest moments of your life God intended for good?

And what if the purest moments of bliss contained your greatest contributions to this world?

God speaks through story because that is how we best understand the most important things.

ARROWS POINTING

That arrow we talked about—the one we're each a pixel in—is a fluid line symbolizing motion, a line that technically has no end. An arrow points to something. It leads to something. So if we are not by accident, and the events of our lives are not accidents either, then it's all leading to something. Take Joseph: he was never in the wrong place at the wrong time, though it must have felt wrong to him (prison?). God was leading him through a series of events that all served great purpose. Even though it was all leading to a specific time and place, it was also building a man God could use.

Sure, our stories lead us toward our purposes, but they also make us into people strong enough to fulfill our purposes.

Brennan Manning wrote,

In a futile attempt to erase our past, we deprive the community of our healing gift. If we conceal our wounds out of fear and shame, our inner darkness can neither be illuminated nor become a light for others. . . . Hope knows that if great trials are avoided great deeds remain undone and the possibility of growth into greatness of soul is aborted.[1]

Margaret was no different than Joseph or Batman or any of us in her calling to tell others' stories. She was shaped by the events of her life; she was moved toward others because of her own suffering; she was most fulfilled investing into the world the deepest needs that had been denied her. God was working for good and even for the saving of lives. Joseph met the need in Egypt and Batman in Gotham City because they had

- the unique gifting to meet the need;
- compassion and character that comes through suffering;
- the right people in their paths;
- the gift of turning up in all the right places, even if they all felt wrong;
- and a passion to see it through.

I know that your story is sacred; maybe the most sacred pieces of you lie there. I'm asking you to dig up the most painful moments of your life, and as I said, I wish I could be physically beside you as you do this. I also know that memories are often more foggy than clear. And I also know that you may not see the point yet.

To build a picture of your story—the events that have shaped you—is a powerful and beautiful thing. It's the darkest and most beautiful moments lined up on an arrow. You will see things you have never seen before.

In a bed-and-breakfast in the middle of nowhere, as Zac and I laid out the moments that had meant the most to us and the moments that had hurt the worst, we were both quiet; but my heart was racing. I started to see something. I started to see that every painful and beautiful thing was moving me somewhere . . . that the most heart-wrenching things were birthing something. I couldn't deny it.

I could look back and for the first time see that the sparks of my greatest passions were lit and fed in these moments. I didn't know exactly where they were taking me, but I could see they weren't by accident. This was a good story—possibly even a great one.

DIFFICULT SONGS

On a Sunday right before Sarah's stroke, with her drowning in the divorce that she had fasted and prayed would not happen, she and I sat together in church. I could feel her crying beside me and she could feel me crying. But we sang. Hands raised. Tears falling. We sang these words together:

> *Bless the Lord, O my soul . . .*
> *Whatever may pass, and whatever lies before me*
> *Let me be singing when the evening comes.*[2]

I don't know what may pass or what lies before you, but I pray we find bigger reasons to sing, no matter the story, "Bless the Lord, O my soul." Perhaps he is teaching us to sing through the pain and joy as he makes something beautiful from it all.

Sarah bounced out her door with her computer as I dropped off something at her house one afternoon last winter. She was nervous about sending out Christmas cards; her unwanted divorce was almost final. It would be the first card without her husband. She turned her computer around, revealing a sad random collaboration of iPhone photos of her kids with "Merry Christmas" tucked at the bottom. She asked what I thought. I told her: "It's terrible."

She frowned and then laughed and then looked at her sad little card again and said, "Ugh! I know."

"Why don't you make a statement, Sarah? Everyone you love knows you are going through the hardest year of your life. Go pay some money and get some great photos with your kids, and show everyone who opens that card that God is seeing you all through this. If you are going to send a card, go for it. Tell the world something."

Weeks later, on the day that Sarah had her massive stroke, hundreds of friends and family opened their mailboxes to her Christmas card. It showed beautiful pictures of her children, the kind of expensive pictures that tell stories. And beneath their faces was the verse, "Because your love is better than life, my lips will glorify you" (Ps. 63:3).

She'd told the world something.

Sarah is still singing. Her voice isn't working yet and may never again, but her eyes sing with a peace that none of us understand. And her story is singing as thousands of people are following her recovery; they're watching as her soul blesses the Lord with no voice and a broken body. But her story hints of glory. It hints of the more we all so desperately hope for and sometimes believe really may exist.

YOUR STORY

BIRTH

JOURNAL

---

01 Identify a highlight from each life stage when you felt pleasure in what you were doing. When were moments you remember being proud and satisfied?

EX   *painting with my grandfather*

0–6

7–12

13–18

19–24

25+

THE
PRESENT

02 Identify a memory from each life stage when you remember suffering.

EX	*my parents divorced*
0–6	
7–12	
13–18	
19–24	
25+	

03 Now lay out these moments on your arrow.

CHAPTER 12

THREADS OF GIFTS

Jessica and Hannah pulled their chairs together during our study in Austin. Jessica held the scribbles revealing her most sacred moments closely. As she looked back over the list of times when she had felt God's pleasure and fully satisfied in her life, they all had something to do with a stage. Performing in a school musical, being elected student council president, giving a talk at a leadership summit.

She realized she was about to have to share them with Hannah, whom she barely knew. So she cynically laughed and said, "I am not sure if these moments display my gifts or my selfishness."

I have watched Jessica wrestle internally for clarity of purpose for years. Yet when that girl prays or teaches, the whole room worships. She exudes an authentic passion. And yet Jessica is terrified of herself. She is gifted—a leader, a teacher, a visionary—but she is only barely using her gifts because of many distinct fears. As we sat together digging up all her fear, she boiled it down for me.

She is afraid if she runs too fast with her strengths as a single woman, that men will find her too strong—too abrasive. She is afraid of dreaming and trying and facing failure or disappointment. She is afraid of her own selfish ambition or the sin that may come out if she really pursued opportunities to use her gifts. She wonders if God made a mistake. Why would he give a woman all this strength?

That night Hannah looked at her and said, "These moments that you feel so happy . . . performing and leading—those would be my worst nightmares. Your pleasure in those moments, God has put that in you."

Jessica called me later to say, "For some reason I thought everyone craved a stage. Maybe I have a responsibility to quit being afraid of my motives and start using the gifts and passions God has put in me."

We tell ourselves it is right to be afraid. I don't know what your fears are, but I know if they aren't from God they are from the enemy, and they need to be taken apart.

Jessica is super analytical, and so am I, and so are a lot of you. We often overanalyze clear simple truths. We tell ourselves it is right to be afraid. I don't know what your fears are, but I know if they aren't from God they are from the enemy, and they need to be taken apart.

We are all unique and needed in this plan. To hide our gifts, or to deny them, or to compare and wish them away is not only taking from yourself; it is taking from God, his church, and a world that needs to see the expression of God you bring. It's the expression he designed you to bring to it.

CREATED TO RUN

In the past month, I have somehow ended up with my kids driving go-carts in two different settings. The first track was at GattiTown;

it was a track the size of a small swimming pool. The cars didn't go anywhere; they just bumped into each other in this little, contained, suffocating circle of a track. It wasn't a track—it was a parking lot. It cost about one dollar, and after my kids finished, they hopped off and ran to the next thing. They didn't even look back.

And then one night while Zac was traveling, I needed to get my little people out. I researched go-carts and found a new track just outside of town. I threw everyone in the car, and we drove to this huge warehouse. We walked in and they issued us helmets and wanted to know if we had any heart conditions. *Ummm . . . where the heck are we?* Then the man behind the register reported that the final tally of our crew's adventure would add up to over a hundred dollars. We had driven all this way. Thankfully, my two youngest were too short for what was about to happen anyway.

To prevent utter devastation, I painfully paid for only my eleven- and thirteen-year-olds' passes. And the two little ones and I took our seats in the bleachers to watch the most incredible race play out. They were strapped in, and they hit their pedals and chased each other at ungodly speeds around more than a mile of track. They were completely free and brave and racing, and I could barely breathe watching them.

It was the most epic go-cart track I'd ever seen.

They did bump into each other occasionally and into the side rails too, but for the most part they just raced their guts out, staying on track and having the time of their lives. They'll never forget that race.

I think most of us have paid a dollar and found ourselves in some stagnant rubber car, bumping into each other.

But what if . . .

What if the things you love to do collided with God's will?

What if you have God-given gifts and he wanted to turn you loose with them?

What if you were built for a track and you are camped out in a parking lot?

I have talked to so many people who are driving around a parking lot, and they can't figure out why they feel so discontent. But they are afraid that if they pull out onto a real track:

They wouldn't actually have anything to contribute.

They would go too fast—get out of control.

They would lose.

They would wreck.

People would judge them.

Joseph had a crazy dream. He was a young man, and he told his brothers that they were going to bow down to him. He was very clear in his gifts. He knew he could interpret dreams. He knew that when he was interpreting that it was from God, and he knew what it meant. And he knew that it was supposed to come true. He thought his gifts, and that even God, were all about his own glory.

Joseph was a bit immature with his gifts in the beginning—he probably shouldn't have rubbed a dream like that in his older brothers' faces. I picture this as a parking-lot season for him. He was brash and arrogant, using his God-given gift for his own purposes. He was crashing into his brothers with it. On that day in his teens when his vision first came to him, clear and happy and with fame and glory, he was all in. He loved it; it was awesome. He was going to change the world, and they were all going to bow down to him. It was a good day—one you may have tasted, with rare moments of vision and clarity when you see your gifts. You have a vision, and then . . . silence.

Twenty years of waiting were coming for him, with no whisper of that vision. No one was bowing down. In fact, the opposite—he was dishonored, mocked, hated. In the wait, Joseph had to decide if he loved God no matter what. No matter what his story was, what his circumstances were. Was he staying in with this God?

I am beginning to think God's favorite word in the entire universe is *wait*. He doesn't use it a lot in the Bible, but we all know it's true. He loves to make us all wait. There is a season for everything, and racing fast around a track with your gifts and vision in Technicolor may not be for today. But he is working in the waiting.

I am beginning to think God's favorite word in the entire universe is wait.

There is a purpose for all of this; there is a track with side rails; there is a reason God gives us gifts. We will experience the pleasure of racing while God is using us, but our gifts' primary purpose is for the building up of others. This may mean a God-given season in the parking lot.

We will look at God's design for all of us to participate as different parts of one body. But there is no entitlement in it. Read what Paul said right after he told us we are each gifted uniquely:

> If I speak in the tongues of men or of angels, but do not have love, I am only a resounding gong or a clanging cymbal. If I have the gift of prophecy and can fathom all mysteries and all knowledge, and if I have a faith that can move mountains, but do not have love, I am nothing. If I give all I possess to the poor and give over my body to hardship that I may boast, but do not have love, I gain nothing. (1 Cor. 13:1–3)

It could be that our time in the parking lots of life is meant to teach us to love. There are often long, drawn-out seasons of waiting between recognizing our gifts and using them to their full potential. And there are often painfully long seasons of time between the glimpse of a vision and its fulfillment.

NATURAL ABILITIES AND SPIRITUAL GIFTS

Every one of us has natural abilities we are born with and spiritual gifts we are given when we become a believer and are filled and empowered by the Spirit.

Back to the story about me at nine years of age with my hands in the carpet, reflecting on leading my cousins in a silly little home-made Christmas pageant. At that time in my life, I was not filled with God's Holy Spirit. Ironically, as we retold the Christmas story, I had not yet seen my own need for the Savior I knew so much about. But God had already placed in me natural abilities as an expression of his creativity. It was part of his plan to someday use my little gifts and my personality and my work to display himself to my little portion of the world. "Every good and perfect gift is from above, coming down from the Father of the heavenly lights" (James 1:17).

At the moment I was saved and filled with the Spirit at seventeen years old, every natural, God-given ability transformed and expanded into one new focus. God took my natural ability to lead, and I gathered younger girls and began to teach my Bible. Strike that—I preached my Bible. I had a new, supernatural gift of teaching. I had never seen it before, and it just poured out of me.

So now my natural abilities were being used supernaturally for God's purposes, and the Spirit was giving me a new gift that I could use to show his glory more fully on this earth.

Let me be clear: I can look back now in my midthirties and see this. At the time, I was uncertain and insecure, and I had no idea what the words *spiritual gifts* even meant. I can promise you, my gifts were wild and undeveloped—for crying out loud, I was seventeen. So before you picture magical moments that cause envy, hear that this has been a lifelong journey of discovering and growing in a gifting. Some of you have hints of your gifts, or maybe it is perfectly clear to you, or maybe you think you have nothing good to offer.

We are going to dig a little. We are going to get under the hood and see what is in you. What has God given you to bring him glory here?

What are you just flat great at? I mean, don't go all spiritual on me. Are you a great storyteller, or are you funny, or are you a musician or great at math or problem solving or listening or running? Or are you good with your hands, like all Pinterest crafty? I don't like you if you are that good at that kind of stuff, but I get that you can't help it. My sister and my mom are brilliant party hosts and chefs and homemakers and designers. I fight jealousy and inadequacy as I stir powdered pink lemonade in a plastic yellow pitcher for my kind of hostessing, but whatever.

For just a moment, compare yourself to no one else and lay down every picture of what you think it looks like to be gifted for God. Think about what you love and what you are great at. If you are a believer in Jesus, this may be how God's Spirit has gifted you to build up his church.

THE PLEASURE OF GOD

Eric Liddell was born in 1902, the son of missionaries in China. His story is retold in the film *Chariots of Fire*. Eric felt called to give his life to God, and in that pursuit he trained and planned to become a missionary, like his parents. But Eric had a gift. He could run, and every door was opening for him to do it. Doors opened all the way to the Olympics. As the film portrays Eric processing his calling and his gifts with his sister, he says these famous words: "I believe God made me for a purpose, but he also made me fast. And when I run I feel his pleasure."[1]

Some of us are hung up on looking for super spiritual gifts like prophecy or healing. But what if you are just fast? What if you are a great musician? What if you excel at accounting? What if you feel God's pleasure as you design buildings or format PTA calendars?

When do you feel God's pleasure?

The answer to this question will help you determine the unique things he has given you to use while you are here. There is no spiritual and secular divide. We have built these divisions.

There is no spiritual and secular divide. We have built these divisions.

"Whatever you do, do it all for the glory of God" (1 Cor. 10:31). Even the seemingly small and boring parts that may not seem spiritual.

We are all given things so that we might show God to others. The raw materials of our lives will come together and be used to bless others and build God's kingdom.

GIFTS

JOURNAL

Looking back over your story from chapter 11, process those
moments again and define what about those moments was so
fulfilling.

An example: My friend Jessica remembers painting with her
grandfather as so fulfilling as a child because she felt she could
express her emotions through art and she felt understood by him.

So several unique things about Jessica would be that she has a
high value for

creating
expressing herself
being understood and understanding

Built into our most fulfilling moments are our most unique
contributions to this world.

YOUR MOMENTS	WHY YOU FELT SATISFIED

CHAPTER 13

THREADS OF SUFFERING

Out of our pain we will heal our world. This isn't a trite saying; it is truth. Because whatever we failed to receive as children are the very things we most want to give. So we don't dig up the past without just cause. We dig up the past because it is some of the most fertile material in our lives.

I live in Austin, and all of my friends have compost piles. If you don't know what that is, just think third-world slums in the corner of your suburban backyard. Any waste in your home that can decompose you put out there: banana peels, pizza crust, coffee grounds . . . and if you are really lucky you have a pet who contributes his waste. Okay—clear enough.

Austin is a tolerant environment. The assortment of alternative lifestyles in our neighborhood is unending, but the one singular intolerable Austin sin is the absence of a compost pile. Nevertheless, I will not relent. I will not be all things to all people. Plus it's gross, and I don't grow things. See, most everyone accompanies their compost pile with a lovely, frugal little vegetable garden. Their compost is the most fertile soil; Miracle-Gro can't compete with this stuff, so they say.

The messiest waste of our lives becomes the most fertile soil.

My childhood family was the idyllic picture of my parents' generation of the American dream. My parents were involved socially and at church, and they were raising three girls who behaved and appeared to love God. My dad tucked us in every night on his knees and prayed for us beside our beds. But somehow, amid all the good, I grew up feeling like I could never reach an invisible moving mark, and it haunted me. The pain of that chased me into adulthood and seemed to grow, not fade.

Approval was oxygen, and many times it felt as if I could not breathe.

Fathers and mothers seem to contain the power to accidentally crush their children with nothing but words.

Oh, the grace I have now that I am a parent. We are just going ahead and setting the money aside for our kids' counseling funds.

But as a child there is no perspective, just fear and pressure and trying to measure up, feeling like I never could. I wanted nothing more than for my dad to unconditionally and recklessly love me, and I thought I could perform well enough to earn that.

No one was dead or divorced or bankrupt. There are so many more dramatic, painful moments from my life I could share, but this particular ache, this chase, contained my greatest fear and my greatest pursuit.

Years later my dad would apologize for the hurts this caused in my childhood. At that time he shared about the hurts from his childhood full of similar pressure and inadequacy. Our struggles almost always take root in our childhoods, and those struggles can go on to entangle us our entire lives. Or, if we are brave enough to face them, they could be the greatest weapons we have to help set others free.

The deep holes I was working to fill would eventually define what I would most desire to give away to the world.

What are your holes? I remember watching an interview with Steven Curtis Chapman and his brave wife, Mary Beth, following the tragic death of their youngest daughter, Maria. Mary Beth spoke of many people coming up to her and telling the amazing ways God was using her daughter's death. She quickly and painfully told the interviewer, "I don't care if this is for God's glory—she was my daughter."[1]

What she spoke in that moment captivated the world, because anyone who has truly suffered has fought the same fight with God, thinking, *God, you must be cruel to allow hell to pour down on us for your name's sake.*

Is he cruel, or does he live with a perspective that we can't conceive?

In the very best of stories there is a moment that is so dark you are unsure how the characters or your own soul will ever recover. *Braveheart, Titanic,* even *Peter Pan.* You can't see the road out when everyone is tied up and about to die. Very few cruel stories ever leave you there, but the best of stories always go there.

CHANGED OR CRUSHED

Gilbert Tuhabonye grew up in Burundi. Similar to my son's neighboring Rwanda, it is a country familiar with tribal war. Gilbert was given a gift like Eric Liddell's; he was fast. He ran to get water, he ran five miles to and from school, and he ran to feed his family's cows. In school, Gilbert began to run competitively, with realistic aspirations of running in the Olympics.

But on October 21, 1993, a tribal war was reawakened between the Hutus and Tutsis. Gilbert and more than a hundred of his Tutsi classmates and teachers were forced into a classroom, where many were beaten and burned to death. Nine hours later, Gilbert would miraculously crawl out from under his friends' charred bodies, badly burned himself, and run through the night toward a future that he could never have imagined.

I know most of you reading this have not tasted suffering like Gilbert's. But I also know that every one of you reading this has tasted some version of suffering. We live in a broken world, and it's just overflowing with it.

We are all tempted to shut down when the fire gets too hot. But who would not lie under his friends' bodies and wish to die? Who would be brave enough to dig out and run? That's crazy, and yet that same passion is in us.

We can do one of two things with suffering: we can absorb it and let it change us, or we can let it crush us.

Suffering will change you, or it will crush you.

Suffering will change you, or it will crush you.

I know people to whom it's done both. Honestly, on a given day, it does both to me at the same time. We're building the stories of our lives—the highest points and the lowest points. Something about the highest points reveals what it is we were made to do that brings God pleasure.

But it is trickier to consider that God knew about every single darkness that you would face before you ever faced it. Every single one. He knew it. I don't say that lightly or without a lot of fear and trembling, because I know some of you are dealing with unthinkable hurt.

GOD HIDES HERE

God didn't let Joseph just be sold into slavery so he could get to Egypt; he had Joseph's brothers do it. He could have found another way. But God absolutely devastated Joseph. For twenty years, the only people who had really known him before he was a nameless slave wanted him dead.

So Joseph was stuck in a life of slavery and prison, and outside of that life there was no hope of an earthly family who loved him. A person in prison who has no one on the outside—not one other person on earth who cares if he is alive . . . What does that force someone to do?

Often that person cries out to God and seeks to know him. I'm watching it in Sarah right now. She can't talk to anybody but God, so as I tell her that we all can see she is so close to God right now, she cries. When you don't have anything or anyone else on earth, all of a sudden God starts looking really good. Something about us needs to long for heaven. When everything is right and everything works—be honest, we don't long for heaven or for God. We just don't.

When you don't have anything or anyone else on earth, all of a sudden God starts looking really good.

We live differently when we are crushed. Arrogance is born when there is no crushing. We need to want Jesus. God knows that. There is not one part of you that he dismisses. There is not one tear you will ever cry that is not felt deeply by God. But he is not afraid to let us suffer. We can't get away from it.

Paul said, "We boast in the hope of the glory of God. Not only so, but we also glory in our sufferings, because we know that suffering produces perseverance; perseverance, character; and character, hope" (Rom. 5:2–4).

Before we get bitter and ask how this could happen, how God could ever say that unimaginable suffering is worth it, look what Paul made clear in the next verses: "And hope does not put us to shame, because God's love has been poured out into our hearts through the Holy Spirit, who has been given to us" (v. 5).

You see, at just the right time, when we were still powerless, Christ died for the ungodly. "Very rarely will anyone die for a righteous person, though for a good person someone might possibly dare to die. But God demonstrates his own love for us in this: While we were still sinners, Christ died for us" (vv. 7–8).

Paul quickly warns us not to question God's love, because God chose the worst kind of suffering because of his love for us!

But we still come back to the question, why does God let us suffer?

Jesus is best known through suffering.

Every time I want to be mad at God because of suffering, he shows me Jesus. As the Bible puts it, "I want to know Christ—yes, to know the power of his resurrection and participation in his sufferings" (Phil. 3:10). And it is true: I have known Jesus most deeply in suffering. He seems to inhabit suffering, and he endured it too. He is not a God unfamiliar with suffering, and he is near our broken hearts.

We get stronger.

With suffering comes a morbid but helpful perspective that life is moving fast and this earth is not our home. I used to live in fear that my life wasn't going to work out just right. The more I surrender to suffering, and to joy, and to whatever God has for me, the less I worry about that. Now my biggest fear is that I won't spend my life well for God. I can run farther and longer than I could before. I am not despairing; faith is growing.

We hurt for heaven.

Hours ago we sat at a funeral for a friend who committed suicide. Yesterday the state of Oklahoma nearly blew away in tornados. And today is one of those days you just hurt for heaven. After twenty-four hours of scenes of flattened neighborhoods and missing children, the whole country is hurting for all the wrongs to be made right and all the shock to be made peaceful.

Suffering often jars us out of comatose lives. As I listened to the pastor describe the life of our friend, I ached to be with him in heaven, and I also ached to live this short life with as much passion and love as humanly possible.

Suffering reminds us this life is short, and this earth is not our home.

> Dear friends, do not be surprised at the fiery ordeal that has come on you to test you, as though something strange were happening to you. But rejoice inasmuch as you participate in the sufferings of Christ, so that you may be overjoyed when his glory is revealed. (1 Peter 4:12–13)

His glory will be revealed, and those who have suffered most will be the most overjoyed.

Our lives could leave a mark.

If we are here for just a breath, I'd like my one little breath to feel more like a mighty gust of wind. That takes surrender, perseverance, and not wasting my minutes away on comparing or complaining. The apostles walked away from painful persecution, "rejoicing because they had been counted worthy of suffering" (Acts 5:41).

It is an honor to suffer. It is a privilege. And we are not to waste it. God wrote suffering into our stories and wants to redeem it for his glory. And if we weren't shaking our fists at him, we could possibly sit down and see that we are running from a life in flames toward a great purpose—a purpose that could never exist without the flames.

He says, *I want to redeem your suffering into beautiful things. I can make beautiful things out of ashes. Nobody else can do that. I can. I can turn dead and dry bones into living life. I can redeem death and make it alive. I can take the most awful, horrific, terrible circumstances and bring life into them.*[2]

How will he do that?

I'll tell you how he has done it in my life.

My dad is better than ever now at telling me how proud he is of me. Looking back, I realize that in spite of his hurtful words so long ago, he has always been proud of me. Because of his own scars, he just didn't know exactly how to show me.

But as a child I could perceive only that my worst fear was coming true. The very thing my soul craved more than any other was out of my reach . . . my daddy's approval.

And like all bondage, my quest for my dad's approval turned into pleasing anyone I could. And eventually I found myself in complete bondage. I was not free. I was motivated, but the motive of my heart, the song I sang in my head, my thoughts, the way I interacted with people, what I thought about when I woke and when I lay down, was all about trying to please people around me. I was completely chained up.

God used something dark to break chains in me and to set me free. I stood staring my worst fear in the face, and God has never felt closer.

If our worst fears come true . . . God. And as we suffer and he comforts us, we comfort others.

Second Corinthians 1:3–4 says, "Praise be to the God and Father of our Lord Jesus Christ, the Father of compassion and the God of all comfort, who comforts us in all our troubles, so that we can comfort those in any trouble with the comfort we ourselves receive from God."

My freedom and the way God filled my soul lit in me a passion, which eventually turned into a calling. Everywhere I go I see people stuck in bondage to something invisible, and I lose sleep, pound the table, and spend endless hours fighting for their freedom through writing and teaching.

Out of my pain, I see others' pain, and because I have tasted freedom I crave others' freedom.

Abortion recovery groups . . .

Words penned on how to walk through a divorce you never wanted . . .

Crying with your friend who just lost her mother . . .

A friend sharing for the first time that she was abused because you just shared your abuse . . .

Moving toward caring for the fatherless through adoption because you never had a father . . .

Out of our pain, we heal. Out of our bondage, we set free.

And again, the messiest waste of our lives becomes the most fertile soil.

I'm getting there, embracing suffering. But as I embrace it, it seems only to increase. It helps to read Genesis 50, where Joseph faced his brothers who had caused decades of suffering to him and said, "What you intended to harm me, God meant it for good." Then he said, "For the saving of many lives."[3]

Our suffering could possibly save lives. If God's arrow really does go on forever and ever and never ends, it's justifiable that God cares more about our eternity with him than this little pixel today.

After we studied suffering together in Austin, a woman wrote to me who had been abused as a child, physically and sexually. She said, "I have never thought that those dark moments could ever be used for good until today. And with that thought my soul healed a little more."

FIRES BURNING

Gilbert from Burundi is still running. I see him run, because he lives in my neighborhood with his two daughters and his wife, Triphine. Gilbert was given the opportunity to train for the Olympics in the United States and was awarded a scholarship to Abilene Christian University. He built Gilbert's Gazelles, the premier training group for runners and triathletes in Central Texas, into one of the most respected runners' training groups in the country, and he cofounded the Gazelle Foundation, whose mission is to build water projects in Burundi. He travels and speaks, sharing his scars so that he can share God's story.

As a young boy in Burundi he learned a saying: "It is easy to light a fire and difficult to extinguish it." He wrote in his memoir, "I understand that saying much better now than I did. Though some would have liked to see me destroyed by flames, no one can extinguish the fire inside of me. The light God placed there still burns brightly." And then he wrote, "I must go run now."[4]

What men meant for evil, God meant for good, for the saving of many lives. Fires are lit in our lives, and they can burn to shine light or cause destruction. We get to decide which purpose they will serve.

SUFFERING

YOUR MOMENTS	WHY IT WAS PAINFUL

JOURNAL

Look back at chapter 11 to the most difficult moments of your
life. I want to be sensitive to your processing. If you just wrote
down things you have never shared with anyone or if you are
still deeply grieving a loss or abuse, this project may be too
difficult right now. It may be helpful to process this project with
a trusted friend.

How have these moments shaped your life?

Write some possible ways God could use
each experience to help someone else.

Do your best to identify five keywords from this page that best
identify how your suffering drives some of your passions.

CHAPTER 14

THREADS OF PLACES

Several years ago, I was introduced to Katie Davis through her blog. She's a young twentysomething who was spending her life adopting orphaned girls off the streets of Uganda. Anyone who encounters her life and words goes on to be changed. So our community began to pray about moving to Africa and adopting dozens of children. (Someday I may write a book that does not include a mention of Katie Davis, but when a moment or a person forever changes the way you view God and the way you live life, it seems to keep coming up.)

Bekah is my spunky, passionate friend who would strip down and offer a homeless person her shirt without thinking, if asked. So of course Katie's story had Bekah ready to take her three young babies across the world. But at least at that time, Brandon, her husband, wasn't so sure that stripping in public or the continent of Africa were in their future. So Bekah began to pray, and within days of that surrendered prayer she found herself in a coffee shop sharing Christ with a young woman who worked in Brandon's office. A few weeks later, she was inviting neighbors to a Bible study in her home. Now, three years later, she can look back and see a trail of loved and changed neighbors and coworkers.

She has used the words *my Africa* many times to reference her neighborhood and Brandon's workplace.

Marc and Kayan also met Katie Davis through her blog around the same time we did. They were new believers who had originally attended our church because of its many adoptive families with kids from Rwanda. They were adopting from Rwanda too. They say, "Some people find adoption through God. We found God through adoption."

Marc and Kayan sat in the same seats with Brandon and Bekah while my husband preached surrender, and all of our community prayed about their personal "Africa." Marc, a respected physician in Austin, began to envision taking his skills in internal medicine and their three babies to Rwanda to train doctors and offer health care to a country in desperate need of it. Kayan was on board. They sold their house in one of the nicest neighborhoods in Austin and are now preparing for their move to Rwanda in the coming months.

There is no escaping this question if we are going to look at purpose:

Do we stay in our place, or do we need to go? Place is so important to our purpose; it determines the environment that nourishes us and the people we come into contact with. Katie probably could not have had the same impact in Alaska, say. Bekah's gifts were perfectly suited for right where she was. So what about your place?

Some of you have jobs you hate and will be called to stay, and some of you have jobs you love and God will call you to go. The paradigm of a believer is holistically different than that of those without God. Without a living God, you get to be your own god. With a living God, who works for eternal purposes, he gets to use us however he pleases.

BE THERE

Let's start with what we can know. We know our mission is to know God and make him known. We know at least a glimpse of the story of God through Scripture. We know we are to love, without warrant, every person God puts in our paths. And we know we are to love God more than all of it. You'll remember that though we may not know God's specific, detailed will for us, 99 percent of being in the will of God is being wholly willing to be in the will of God.

God is quiet and completely wise in his timing of revealing his will.

Most of you reading this have enough opportunity for ministry right under your noses that you never need to move or change a thing. In Austin there is a bumper sticker floating around that says, "Life is too short to live in Dallas." Austinites think it's funny. Here is my version for our purposes today: Life is too short to spend much time worrying about where on this planet you should be. As Jim Elliott, the great martyr missionary said, "Wherever you are, be all there."[1]

God is quiet and completely wise in his timing of revealing his will.

We live in a space in history where job changes, moves, and relocations are within reason and perfectly acceptable. So rather than be paralyzed with fear that you may move when you should have stayed or you may stay when you should have moved, pray and commit your ways to the Lord. And then go *do something*.

God asks us into his will like a loving dad in a swimming pool, asking his little child to jump. Whether that child jumps really far or barely scoots on his bottom into the pool, that dad will move to catch him. So don't be afraid. God's will is moving, and if we will just jump, his will is going to catch us. Let him be God; move on with what you know and quit overanalyzing what you don't.

> Do not be anxious about anything, but in everything, by prayer and petition, with thanksgiving, present your requests to God. And the peace of God, which transcends all understanding, will guard your hearts and your minds in Christ Jesus. (Phil. 4:6–7)

Joseph did this so beautifully. God had shown him he would do these awesome things with his life, and rather than worry about being stuck in prison or as a slave, he did great things wherever he was.

Do great works wherever you are. Likewise, do not be afraid to go or do not be afraid to stay.

Let him be God; move on with what you know and quit overanalyzing what you don't.

We line up lives in order of splendor or impact or performance, but God is after his glory. In heaven, Katie Davis won't be rewarded because of her location on earth; she will be rewarded for her obedience and faithfulness. And those who spent most of their lives in cubicles and driving Suburbans in carpool lines will be standing beside her receiving similar crowns.

It's not our place; it's what we do in our places.

Joseph had a determination that is missing in our generation. Not to put too fine a point on it, but I think we are a bunch of wimps. In general, we try our best to avoid difficult work. But when Joseph was in slavery and in prison, he picked up the mop and said, "Okay, I'm going to work with this. I'm going to make the best of this." That's powerful.

With no explanation from God as to why his life was in ruin, he made a choice to be a kick-butt slave. He was awesome. He gave his life to it, without any entitlement, without any complaining. He did his best so much that he was promoted to running his owner's home and leading the prison.

So if we know no place, no job, no marriage, no child is going to fulfill us perfectly, we can make the choice to quit fighting for happiness in all of it and start to fight for God's glory in it.

For Joseph, his fulfillment was a determination and a choice that certainly took conscious initiation. He gave everything he had to serve well, even as a slave and a falsely accused inmate. So if we know no place, no job, no marriage, no child is going to fulfill us perfectly, we can make the choice to quit fighting for happiness in all of it and start to fight for God's glory in it.

It takes a determination every day to trust him while you're still in your place.

JUMPING INTO PLACE

After Christ gave the Great Commission and ascended to heaven, the apostles got after it and were persecuted as they went. The apostle Paul wrote this from prison in Philippians 1:

> Now I want you to know, brothers and sisters, that what has happened to me has actually served to advance the gospel. As a result, it has become clear throughout the whole palace guard and to everyone else that I am in chains for Christ. And because of my chains, most of the brothers and sisters have become confident in the Lord and dare all the more to proclaim the gospel without fear. (vv. 12–14)

What Paul was saying is basically this: "I am preaching the

gospel to the world from a prison cell. I'm doing my job, what he put me on earth to do, wherever I am. But I'm also representing Christ, even if I'm not preaching to somebody. Even when I'm not writing an epistle to you, everybody in this prison is watching me in chains. How I live day in and out in these chains is changing them."

Why don't we see our jobs, our blogs, our neighborhoods, or even our time in hospitals or infertility clinics like this? Often we applaud exceptional ministry and miss the everyday ministry that nobody sees.

What Paul and Joseph both assumed was that somehow, in their God-given places, God was most effectively able to preach the gospel. I want you to ask yourself that question about your place. Are you set in the places you are in because that is the most strategic place for you to preach the gospel? Let me tell you what happens when you start to think that way. Everything changes.

You change the question from: "Are my neighborhood, my workplace, my school, and my life stage making me happy?" to: "Are my neighborhood, my workplace, my school, and my life stage the most strategic places for my kids, my life, my story, my personality, and everything I need to preach the gospel?"

I have watched some of you actually come to a good answer to the first question because you quit asking it and simply considered the bigger question.

I remember Rachel, my friend who is an occupational therapist, telling me one night that she wanted to start praying for her coworkers. It wasn't even sharing her faith; it was just praying. And somehow, a week later, at a bar during happy hour after work, one of her coworkers, Amanda, asked her about God. Amanda and her husband went on to receive Christ and are both now leading in our church. And they went on to share Christ beside Rachel with many other coworkers.

All Rachel did was open her eyes in her place to the need that was screaming all around her.

Your place is not an accident; it is by design.

One night, Zac and I found ourselves absorbed in the documentary *Babies*. The documentary follows the first year of life of four babies in different parts of the world.

There is no talking and no real plot, but you *can't quit watching*! An African baby crawling through the mud outside his hut, a baby in urban Tokyo juggling the pressures of, you know, being a baby in urban Tokyo, a Mongolian farm baby taking a bath with the family goat, and an American "green" baby living the life of a hippie.

I shudder to think how accidental we all believe life is.

Watching these babies come into their spots on the planet, you cannot help but think, *There are no accidents or coincidences.* There is a God setting us in our times and our places with our people. And if that is true, he has a plan for it all.

I shudder to think how accidental we all believe life is.

Recently, I was with a girl who wept because she wanted a life of purpose. I asked what she did for a living, and she told me she was developing a sex-education program that might be used in all of the Texas school districts. *Um* . . . I was confused. How could she not feel purpose in that God-given place? She went on to realize there was incredible purpose, but she was living in so much fear that she might fail at this huge task that she couldn't embrace it.

Maybe you are exactly in the will of God, living a life of purpose, but you can't even see it because you are afraid.

Afraid your place doesn't matter.

Afraid you won't succeed.

Afraid God doesn't see you.

Afraid that what you're doing isn't ministry.

Afraid of what people will think if you live for Christ in your place.

OUR REAL PLACES

Your gifts and stories will be used in many different places over the course of your life. We have freedom to dream about our places, and there is great purpose in using our gifts in corporations, non-profits, state school systems, churches, and neighborhoods.

I think some of you could be happy in your place if you thought that, to some degree, God was proud of you right in the midst of your non-African, mundane, punching-numbers job. We all have threads he wants to spin into stories that last forever, and our places are part of that.

Because, you know, we aren't really in our "place" yet. The place we were made for is coming; no place feels quite right until we are home.

PLACES

Name your places in the circles. For example: work, school, neighborhood, dorm, social media.

YOU

JOURNAL

Lay each place before God. Are you supposed to stay there? Likely
yes, but Zac and I do this regularly with our kids' school or with
jobs or church. It keeps our hands open.

Dream with each place. Beside each place write thoughts about
how you could live more intentionally in your places.

What about your places makes you afraid?

CHAPTER 15

THREADS OF PEOPLE

I want to tell you more about my good friend who has died twice. Julie Manning was resuscitated both times, but due to a heart condition, could die again at any point. She doesn't live like anyone else I know. She doesn't waste time with small talk. No one wastes time with Julie, because when you're eating Mexican food on her deck, life feels short.

Julie is thirty-five and has two young boys who know how to dial 911. But Julie is not afraid. She teaches us to not fear death. People who have died get to tell us to be afraid or not.

The day we thought Sarah Henry would go to Jesus, Julie sat beside her bed whispering secrets of hope and life after death. She whispered her memories.

"Sarah, there is complete light and complete peace. You will not worry about your children. You will not fear anything. You will just feel completely overwhelmed by the presence of God. Do not be afraid, friend."

Sarah was about to die, they said, within that day. When Julie walked out of her room, she tucked herself in a corner of the waiting room, and I went to hug her as she cried. When I asked about her tears, she whispered words I will never get over: "I'm jealous."

As my dear friend lay likely facing God that day, no words could ever have comforted me more. Heaven and God aren't myths to Julie; she has tasted them. So every moment we are together we make the very most of it.

Every one of us has people in our lives whom we need and people who need us. Are we intentionally spending our time in those two categories? Or are we casually bumping up against each other with no real purpose to receive or give love?

If we are honest, it is costly to love people. So you know what we do instead of doing the difficult work of loving them? We piddle. We waste the precious time we have. In case you're unfamiliar with the term:

Piddle (v.)
   1. To waste time or spend one's time idly or inefficiently

It is easier to survive this life on the surface, brushing up against people gently, rather than doing the mess of intentionally loving them. Love takes risk. Love takes forgiveness and grace. Love takes effort, time, and commitment. You commit not to bolt when it gets hard, because it will get hard.

And if this is the cost of deep relationship, we just don't have capacity and space to go deep with everyone. So we have to become intentional.

RUNNING PARTNERS

We have talked about the verses in Hebrews 12 that call our lives here a race we're running, and we want to run well. We all forget sometimes that how we run this race matters. So we need people like my friend Julie, who will put their fingers under our chins and lift our heads. I need that perspective in my race. I get tired and want to quit. I need people ahead of me, shouting back that it is worth it. I need deep, kindred souls beside me, making the run more fun and helping me not to feel crazy and alone.

But what's the problem with people?

They are all jacked up. Let me rephrase: *we* are all jacked up. We hurt each other. We let each other down. We disagree. I don't know if a single person with whom I am genuinely close has avoided hurting me. And I guarantee, every person who feels genuinely close to me has been hurt by me too. We are human and flawed—even those who know God.

Accepting that fact allows me to have grace for every other person who comes into my life. If I can accept that I am so sinful and so broken that I am likely to hurt anyone close to me on any given day without even being aware of it, I can willingly pass out grace to those who hurt me. Zac and I save money for our children's counseling, knowing we will mess them up. As a nice gesture, we'll pay for their recovery and show up and apologize when they are eighteen. Because we know good and well we are not perfect parents. We're not a perfect pastor and pastor's wife. We know we're not the best of friends to people. We know that we will fail people over and over again.

If I can truly see that I am completely messed up and that God rescued and saved me from myself, and not because I did anything or deserved it, then there is a complete and utter freedom in my life to issue that same grace to everybody else. I am a rescued mess of a human, and so are you. And we will hurt each other sometimes because that is what jacked-up humans do. But I still need you.

We keep running together, even though we hurt each other.

Julie, with her heart that doesn't work, just ran a marathon, and she asked me to run a mile with her. Just one mile. I said no. Because I knew myself; I run so slowly that I worried I would hold her back.

But Julie didn't want to run with her failing heart alone. We need to run with people, right? But we look around and we only have imperfect people to run with. I should have run with Julie because she asked me. I should have run with her because I love her, and even if I was going to mess her up and slow her down, she would know I love her and know I am committed to her. I should have run.

We must imperfectly run together. Not because we're fast or great at this or because it's always going to work out with a glorious win. But because we are committed to each other.

Here is the thing about Joseph. Joseph stuck it out with his awful people. He committed to them, not because they were good to him, but because they were his people. His brothers stabbed him in the back, selling him into two decades of slavery and prison, and they ended up standing before him in need. He did not just give them what they needed; he gave them everything they could ever want. They were his people and he was all in, no matter what.

Joseph said to his brothers, "I am Joseph! Is my father still living?" But his brothers were not able to answer him, because they were terrified at his presence.

Then Joseph said to his brothers, "Come close to me." When they had done so, he said, "I am your brother Joseph, the one you sold into Egypt! And now, do not be distressed and do not be angry with yourselves for selling me here, because it was to save lives that God sent me ahead of you. . . .

Do this: Load your animals and return to the land of Canaan, and bring your father and your families back to me.

I will give you the best of the land of Egypt and you can enjoy the fat of the land . . ."

Joseph gave them carts, as Pharaoh had commanded, and he also gave them provisions for their journey. To each of them he gave new clothing. (Gen. 45:3–5, 17–18, 21–22)

We have to pick our people and commit to them, expecting they will hurt us but not giving up easily on them when they do.

Joseph could not control his circumstances, but he intentionally leveraged every relationship in his path for the glory of God. He never wasted opportunity to serve, even those who wronged him.

WHO DO YOU NEED?

We don't just need people; we need the right people. Sometimes finding the right people takes discipline and effort. And then when we find them, we have to fight for them. We have to prioritize time and issue grace over and over, because even the best human on this earth will disappoint us. And when that happens, you love and fight for that person even harder.

We have to pick our people and commit to them, expecting they will hurt us but not giving up easily on them when they do.

If any part of you listening to these words right now thinks to yourself, *I don't know if I have enough of the right people in my life,* you probably don't.

We all fell in love with shows like *Friends* because we deeply want to have "our people." Close friends and mentors don't fall in our laps. You search and invest, and then you allow them to be imperfect versions of what you were hoping for in your head. Most of us are waiting to be invited, waiting to be pursued, waiting for friends to come to us. But that's not the way it happens. Instead, the Bible says:

> Put on then, as God's chosen ones, holy and beloved, compassionate hearts, kindness, humility, meekness, and patience, bearing with one another and, if one has a complaint against another, forgiving each other; as the Lord has forgiven you, so you also must forgive. And above all these put on love, which binds everything together in perfect harmony. And let the peace of Christ rule in your hearts, to which indeed you were called in one body. And be thankful. (Col. 3:12–15 ESV)

Love is an active process, and we are fairly lazy. So initiate. Then, when you come together, initiate depth. Great conversations come from great questions and honest answers. One of the ways I grow and experience God is over queso and salsa with kindred friends talking about deep things. It takes initiative to ask deeper questions and sheer bravery to give sincere answers. Pray and find ways to take your friendships to a deeper level.

WHO NEEDS YOU?

Before any knowledge of her faulty heart, Julie trained and became a pediatric cardiology RN. Last week I walked into an enormous room as Julie shared about her heart and death and faith to a room full of men and women in the cardiology community. She has her close people to run beside her in this journey, but she also has her patients and the cardio community. They need to hear hope and believe that there is life after death and a God who has rescued them with the blood of his Son.

Dare you tell me that is all an accident? That she trained to take care of hearts while her own heart was failing and she didn't even know? That she is placed at the bedsides of children who are dying of heart disease and she can tell them about heaven? Tell me it was random coincidence. God placed her in her spot. And Acts 17:27 says, "God did this so that they would seek him and perhaps reach out for him and find him."

He is after the people around you, and he pursues them through us.

He is after the people around you, and he pursues them through us.

I know your life may feel more random and disconnected than Julie's seems, but you cannot hear her story and tell me God didn't orchestrate the good and the bad to intersect. And you also can't tell me he would plan the details of Julie's and Joseph's lives and ignore yours.

Next time you are in a public space, be awkward and look in people's eyes. People—nearly every one of them—are hurting, even if they don't say it. And we hold their cure. We get to give God away, and it is for our joy. I am never more content than when I am meeting needs.

Joseph looked at his brothers and said essentially, "What you meant as harm, God meant for the saving of many lives."[1] Even after all they did to him, he thought it was worth it for people.

At some point we have to decide whether or not it is worth it to spend our lives helping people be free from bondage, meeting their needs, cheering for them as they run, giving them God. And at some point, if I find myself being completely mocked and rejected and hurt, is it still worth it for me?

That is the question we all have to ask. Is it worth the saving of many lives to you?

So who needs God around you?

Pray.

Pursue them.

Ask them great questions.

Share your struggles and your God.

Dream of ways you can meet their needs.

Seek out relationships with people outside of your circles. Some of my favorite moments in my life have happened as I have stepped out of my comfort zone. Like taking some women from a local halfway house out to bowl with some of my friends. I remember sitting in a bowling alley with a woman just out of prison who exuded more joy than I remember ever feeling in my life. She was about to see her kids, and it had been years. Her joy and perspective changed me—and I need to be changed. God's economy makes beautiful exchanges: as we give, we grow.

Seek risks and uncomfortable things. You do not risk like a fool; you are wisely investing in the only two things that will not die: God and people's souls.

God's economy makes beautiful exchanges: as we give, we grow.

But if we keep piddling, we will miss it all.

As Zac and I led and loved our church, some of the people we needed and loved most turned out to be the people who hurt us the most. I remember working to forgive and wondering if it was ever possible. It turns out that loving people recklessly requires hurting deeply. If we didn't love them so much, it wouldn't have hurt so deeply.

But something bigger is going on here. "For our struggle is not against flesh and blood, but against the rulers, against the authorities, against the powers of this dark world and against the spiritual forces of evil in the heavenly realms" (Eph. 6:12). As I read that verse at the time, I lifted up above all the people who hurt us, and I could see so clearly that this wasn't about them and me. There was actually a devil trying to divide us—to crush our relationships, our church. I wasn't fighting them and they weren't fighting me. We were all running, and dark forces were chasing us, tackling us, discouraging us, and doing anything they could to make us check out of this race.

All of a sudden I could forgive. We are not warring against flesh and blood. There is a war, but it isn't against each other. Satan would like us to think that it is.

What Joseph knew, and what you hear in his words over and over again, is to trust in God. This relentless, unconditional trust didn't make sense. "What you did to me? I completely believe, with all of my heart, that God did it. This was not about brothers, favoritism of your father. This was about God. This was about something bigger happening on earth."

INTENTIONAL

Five years before Sarah Henry had her strokes, she sat on my bed and watched me pack for a trip. She was impatient that I was leaving. I was one of her only friends because she had recently moved to Austin. She wondered out loud if she would ever have friends like she had in college. I looked at her and said, "Quit waiting for people to pursue you. They won't. Pursue them."

Outside of the ICU while Sarah was facing death because of her strokes, waiting rooms could not contain us all. Somewhere in the midst of three kids and a busy, full life over those five years, she pursued. She asked great questions and risked vulnerable pieces of herself and spoke about her God to us. She loved well, and many, many people call Sarah friend.

Together, through our suffering and her loss, we are doing our best to give back what she has given us. As she heals, we pray. We pursue. We ask great questions she can't answer with words just yet. We bare our souls while she listens with her whole body and all of her old Sarah personality, and then we give her back the God she gave us so well.

As the world has watched, we've all wondered . . . *If it were us in that bed, have we loved deep enough to have friends like this?*

Sarah, Joseph, and Jesus did not waste time trying to control their circumstances. They invested their time in strategically and unconditionally loving and serving people. It is the best investment of our lives.

PEOPLE

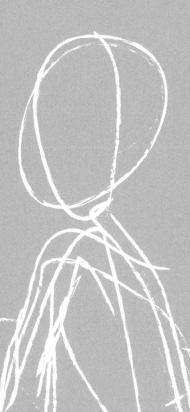

JOURNAL

Dream about the people you need and the people who need you. Write a few names of people you want to be more intentional about spending time with.

PEOPLE YOU NEED

Mentors

Friends

Family

Other

PEOPLE WHO NEED YOU

Neighbors

Coworkers

Friends

Family

Outside of acquaintances
prison, elderly, poor

Other

CHAPTER 16

THREADS OF PASSIONS

William Wilberforce knew his passion. He resisted it, but this passion held him captive as a young man, nearly at the same time that he became completely captivated by Jesus. He met God and wanted nothing more than to begin vocational ministry; he was convinced this was the best way to serve God. But the passion that kept him up at night, that had him pacing floors and banging tables, was the unacceptable injustice of the slave trade in England.

His minister, John Newton, a former slave trader, enlightened him about the horrors of slavery. William was haunted. God had given him a gift for communication, the empathy of one who had suffered, a position of influence through the House of Commons, and a deep, lifelong friendship with the prime minister of England. And he was faced with a need too awful to ignore. A dozen or more threads, ordained by the hand of God, were slowly assembling into a great calling.

Finally, Wilberforce's friends convinced him that God could potentially use him most in the place of politician. He ran headfirst toward the thing that haunted him. It was painful, and most of his life was spent before there was any reform.[1] But at some point his passions turned into a calling. When that happens, the cost becomes irrelevant.

Do you see the need around you?

We often miss this as a main point of the story of Joseph, but it is key. What was God doing through Joseph's decades of suffering? Was he refining Joseph? Yes. Was he restoring Joseph to his family? Yes. But ultimately God intended Joseph's life "to save many lives." And by the end of Joseph's life, he told his brothers it was all worth it.

NEED

Every Christian knows that Christ gives us a foundational calling: to live as Christ. Christ met needs. And all our other passions serve only to lead us to the unique needs we can meet. Wilberforce and Joseph weren't especially spectacular human beings; they just gave their lives to the problems of their generations. We could do that too. And together, as one body with many parts, we could see God move.

The word *passion* originates in Latin, meaning "to suffer." The word was created by religious scholars in the eleventh century to describe the willing suffering of Christ. Passions have become nearly synonymous with pleasures and what excites us in modern culture. But consider that passion is originally defined as the moment of the deepest willing suffering of Christ for our good. It lifts the word from human desires to a monumental love willing to suffer.

When we find ourselves willing to choose suffering for a cause, that cause may hold our life's mission.

God often leads us to passions through suffering, experienced or perceived. As you considered your scars on this journey, hopefully passions began to arise out of your darkest moments. You long to give the world what you failed to receive. Passions are also born out of observing the suffering of others.

God often leads us to passions through suffering, experienced or perceived.

William Wilberforce observed suffering, and as it haunted him, his passions followed with a great intensity that eventually led him to his calling. Joseph suffered great pain in his life, but his suffering gave him a sincere passion for reconciliation and human care. We don't naturally have passion for others; naturally we are dang selfish.

But when we were bought by Christ, we exchanged our hearts full of self-seeking passions for God's heart. And now we share his passions. God said through his prophet,

> I will cleanse you from all your impurities and from all your idols. I will give you a new heart and put a new spirit in you; I will remove from you your heart of stone and give you a heart of flesh. And I will put my Spirit in you and move you to follow my decrees and be careful to keep my laws. (Ezek. 36:25–27)

Our hearts are new, and now what was cold is warm and full of compassion, led and moved by his Spirit.

We were built for this. What begins as a burden and obligation becomes the thing that fills our restless souls.

In the movie *Amazing Grace*, William Pitt's character races through a field with Wilberforce and says to him, "Why is it you only feel the thorns in your feet when you stop running?"[2] When we run for God and for people, we forget for just a moment about ourselves, and it feels amazing. Nothing makes a soul sicker than too much time given to itself.

It's like my five-year-old who I have to force to clean up the back-yard. Every second of it seems to cause him physical anguish, until he finishes and looks up at me and says, "I am good cleaner. That was fun." We aren't ever happy when we're lazy and selfish. The things we often think may steal our joy turn out to be the truest wells of joy that exist.

BEAUTIFUL

Just because God loves us and wanted to make life more fun for us, he built us to love different things so we could meet different needs. So my daughter Kate loves art, and Caroline would rather sing. My son Conner is smarter than most humans on earth, and Coop may be the next Emmitt Smith. And every one of them is permitted to pursue these passions for the glory of God and the love of people.

It's beautiful that your heart doesn't beat fast about the same things my heart beats over. It's beautiful that your gifts are not the same as your mom's, and your place is not the same as your best friend's. When we start to lay out our threads, it is unbelievable—breathtaking, really—to see how what felt average about ourselves weeks ago starts to take on intricate beauty. Our untangling threads reveal God's sovereignty and attention to detail. Beautiful is the body of Christ stretched and poured out into every crevice of this world, every city, every neighborhood, every office, every home. It's the unselfish passions of people displaying the love of their God in a million unique ways. Buechner put it this way: "The place God calls you to is the place where your deep gladness and the world's deep hunger meet."[3]

Beautiful are all your unique threads that cause you to beat the table, or lie in bed awake, or speak with exclamation marks.

As my real-life people in Austin and I worked through this concept in one of my small groups, I glanced down and saw pages of scribbled notes in Amanda's hand. She was all lit up. Amanda was one of the women who had come to know Jesus through Rachel at work, and she was leading one of the groups. She asked her group about the need they saw around them. But it was obvious that Amanda was about to explode, so I turned the question back on her. She went on to tell us about her breakthrough.

Amanda is a speech therapist with Rachel, and she has always known that her work was important to children with fairly severe disabilities, many unable to speak. She went on, "Deep in me, I've known I can communicate, because of my training and gifts, with these kids, sometimes better than even their parents. But this week I heard from a grown man who has the same disability as many of my kids, cerebral palsy. Roger shared how alone he felt in his head because he can't really talk clearly, and how Jesus is the only reason he has not taken his life. It was right in front of me the whole time, but for the first time I thought, *I can tell these kids about Jesus.* So I called Rachel, and together we are going to host a special needs vacation Bible school this summer. Most of these families have never been to church. These kids perhaps have never heard of Jesus."

It was so simple and so beautiful. Her heart was taken captive, haunted by the need in her place, with her people, using her gifts and story of her lifetime without God. And now the Holy Spirit was leading her to her part in his story. Ordinary threads were weaving epic stories. It isn't all as complicated as we often make it.

PASSION KILLERS

Nothing kills passion more than the fear of man, whether a quest for approval or nagging comparison. If we are running our race and our eyes are darting back and forth, we will not see the need around us. Hebrews 12:2 is stern about this. You want to run this race? You fix your eyes on Jesus.

As a young believer, aware of my gifts and increasingly aware of the need around me, I remember passion burning in my chest to teach God to the women around me but thinking to myself, *Why would I ever teach when there are VHS tapes of Beth Moore?*

I compared myself to her rather than fixing my eyes on Jesus. I was distracted from running my race in my place.

Hear me. You have a race that no one else can run. So please run.

"For whatever does not proceed from faith is sin" (Rom. 14:23 ESV). This is a verse that makes every one of us shudder and consider ourselves the worst of sinners. How does everything come from a place of faith? We all doubt and get fearful and wander toward lives completely absorbed with ourselves. We are unable to move without God. He moves us; we just have to let him.

If you are anxious because you don't know your passions or don't know if you are living them or ever could—if you are beating yourself up because you have lived distracted—stop. We will never move forward if

- we cannot love;
- we cannot know God;
- we cannot know ourselves;
- we cannot change;
- we cannot bleed for others.

We can't move without God's Spirit moving in and through us to accomplish his purposes. We are not left as orphans to figure all of this out. He is with us. That is why Jesus could say, "My yoke is easy and my burden is light" (Matt. 11:30). Because he didn't call us to something alone. He carries the yoke for us, so we can run with power.

PASSIONS

YOUR
PASSIONS

JOURNAL

What need do you see around you?

What injustice do you get mad about?

When do you remember meeting a need and feeling very fulfilled?

Write out your greatest passions in the circles. Around each one, jot down
dreams and ways you could engage that passion.

CHAPTER 17

THE TAILOR

Shelby is confident, or so I thought. She was entering her senior year at the University of Texas, and her long blond hair and beautiful smile tricked me, cluttering the truth that she was flat struggling. She was doing her best to smash together a loving God with a broken life. With freshly divorced parents and the heartbreak of a recent breakup, she wanted answers. She sat at my kitchen counter waiting for me to ask her a question that she knew I sincerely wanted the answer to: "How are you?"

Clinging to her coffee cup as I worked on completing dishes, she bravely began to lay out doubts about God and her future. Then she reached for a notebook marked with questions and wrestlings, likely created in the middle of nights with no sleep.

As she glanced at her notes, she fired off questions, most of which I didn't have perfectly wrapped answers for. Then she asked one so close to home, it shook me a little.

"How do I know if I am hearing God?"

It shook me because I was wondering the same thing, and I had felt moved to have company in my search for this answer. God was beginning to lead me toward dreams, but I was terrified they weren't from him. What if I stepped out and it was really just me all along?

The real question we were asking is, "Since God rarely writes in the sky, how do I know what is spiritual and supernatural, and what are just my own futile thoughts?"

Trying to separate human from deity is no small task. It demands knowing God and then digging in the invisible crevice of our souls and Scripture.

From the beginning of this journey, I hope I have been clear that there is no perfect equation leading to clear and fulfilling purpose. And that is in part the brilliance of our God.

WHAT IS MISSING?

Along with most of the world, we have been watching *The Bible* series on the History Channel. Seeing the reality of what these moments may have felt like has changed me. Watching Jesus choose forty days and nights alone with no food or water in the wilderness, all I could think was, *You are God! Why are you doing this to yourself? You do not need extra power when you are the Son of God! Does your Spirit really need to be strengthened and prepared for what is ahead?*

In the series, right after Jesus walks out of the wilderness, having resisted the devil, he prepares to begin his ministry and he closes his eyes. My daughter was watching with me and asked, "Mom, what is he doing?"

I said, "He's praying, baby."

While I have read at least dozens of times that Jesus prayed, to see him pray just broke me down. Our Savior, fully God, depending on his Father for every breath, never acting apart from his Father's will, never acting in his flesh, never bowing down to earthly desires. He wanted so much to live out his Father's will that he subjected himself to forty days without food or water or people. It was so humble and beautiful—God in the flesh . . . dependent.

Jesus knew there was a war, and the war was for us. We were to be won back, and he would choose suffering again and again until he got us back.

His eyes close and Jesus, my Lord and Savior, prays.

I am reminded of the war for my soul—the quiet, subtle, and alluring current pulling me toward doubtful independence. Prayer is hard. It is talking to someone invisible. And it helps to embrace the belief that this invisible God hears me and responds. I am not prone to talking to invisible beings.

If we are all honest, the sin of prayerlessness is common. We have a hard time sitting still with ourselves. We feel restless and cranky, and dealing with God seems daunting. But if we were asked, "Do you pray?" we would all pipe up, "Of course!" Like if someone asked us, "Do you love God?" Of course.

But do we really take chunks of our days and form words in our minds, hearts, and mouths to an invisible God? Or would that "of course" be referring to mealtime or tucking our kids in? Or the tossed up "Thank you, God," as the plane lands on time and intact? Or would that "of course" be a lie, because honestly you can't remember the last time you talked to God? Not about him—to him.

"Never stop praying" (1 Thess. 5:17 NLT). Paul suggests in this verse that our entire lives could and should be lived in belief and dependence on that invisible God. Our generation has so run from the bounds of legalism (which I applaud), that many of us have left behind all the practices designed to help us know and love our God. I want to need prayer and run to it with every discipline and desire.

There are two sides to our war, and while one may be about to win, God is clear that we will personally and daily win only if we cling to him. God's goal for our lives is that we would live in complete and utter surrender and dependence on him. It is always his mercy to show us that need, whatever the cost.

So as each of us processes how we should spend our lives, know that nothing we have done together matters without the Spirit of God. He illumines our understanding of God and of ourselves, and he leads us daily. He empowers every move we will make for his glory. He is God in us, with us, for us, and through us. I do not want to spend one fleeting day here without embracing as much of God as I can.

Jesus said about the Holy Spirit,

> Flesh gives birth to flesh, but the Spirit gives birth to spirit. You should not be surprised at my saying, "You must be born again." The wind blows wherever it pleases. You hear its sound, but you cannot tell where it comes from or where it is going. So it is with everyone born of the Spirit. (John 3:6–8)

When Jesus saves, we have full access to his Spirit. We have a regenerate soul.

Regenerate (adj.)
1. formed or created again
2. spiritually reborn or converted
3. restored to a better, higher, or more worthy state[1]

It is an odd word, but it is one of my favorites because of the fact that the insides of me are completely reborn, new, different. That is the evidence of my salvation; it is the evidence of God in me, and it is the only foundation we can dream of pleasing God from. It takes away the striving and comparing I tend to turn to in this life.

Without a new soul, without the Spirit filling us, we are just jacked-up humans.

But with his Spirit . . .

If we only had an inkling of all we miss because we do not pray, because we do not believe the Spirit in us is able to do impossible things, we would shudder. You have God in you and waiting to go crazy through you, if you would just let him.

After Jesus was raised from the dead, he appeared to his disciples and confirmed what had happened. And he gave clear, convicting instructions: "I am going to send you what my Father has promised; but stay in the city until you have been clothed with power from on high" (Luke 24:49).

This was a big moment. Jesus was telling his men exactly what had just happened and connected it to the prophecies. He was also instructing them how to now proceed. In this one little sentence, there was so much for these men to take in.

NEEDING GOD

We do not have power to change our own souls or to change others. At times that concept has crippled and frustrated me, until its truth shifted to freedom. I do not want to be responsible for what can only be handled and achieved by God himself.

I do not want to be responsible for what can only be handled and achieved by God himself.

It is possible that you have dug into Scripture with all your heart, and prayed for God to show his will, and done every project in this book, and you still feel unsure about your purpose. Take comfort. This is a journey that God put into motion, and he knows us well enough to know that he needs to tether us to himself with the unknowns. We get all independent with what we think we know.

The other day my thirteen-year-old son walked into my room, sat down on the sofa, and said, "Mom, I need to tell you about my day." I immediately assumed he was obligated by the school principal to tell me the trouble he had incurred, but instead he started rambling about his friendships and the girl's heart he recently broke, and he wondered out loud with me how to navigate it all.

My son, for the first time in months, needed me, and he couldn't have done any more spectacular act to show his love for me.

Close your eyes, like Jesus did, and pray. Right now. Wherever you are, tell God you need him. We forget we need him, but he dearly loves to hear from us. And the beautiful thing is that we tend to remember when we are pouring our lives into his purposes. When we are building for him, his Spirit reminds us we need him every day.

I remember I need God when:

I feel tangled up with sin and fear.

> For the Spirit God gave us does not make us timid,
> but gives us power, love and self-discipline. (2 Tim. 1:7)

I don't know what to do.

> My sheep listen to my voice; I know them, and they follow me.
> (John 10:27)

I forget.

> But the Advocate, the Holy Spirit, whom the Father will send
> in my name, will teach you all things and will remind you of
> everything I have said to you. (John 14:26)

I am discouraged.

In the same way, the Spirit helps us in our weakness. We do not know what we ought to pray for, but the Spirit himself intercedes for us through wordless groans. (Rom. 8:26)

We need God when we are restless, bored, numb, cold, selfish, or distracted. It won't be some great vision that will fill our souls; it will be the Spirit of the living God, and him alone.

RUNNING DEPENDENT

Let me tell you about the thirteen-year-old who just melted me with the meanderings of seventh-grade life. He is our oldest son, Conner. He is naturally a pretty gifted athlete. (He can thank God for accessing more of my husband's gene pool while building my son.) He plays just about every sport right now, minus baseball, which I praise God for because baseball is the most boring, time-consuming sport. Football. Basketball. Lacrosse (boys hitting each other with metal sticks). Way better than baseball.

As good as an athlete as Conner is, early in the season of every sport, he thinks too hard. He plays guardedly and watches the clock and the referee, and you can see him thinking about the plays and minding the rules. He plays fearfully and with caution. But then, finally, at some point in every season, he completely lets go and plays his guts out. Then by the last game or two, my son is playing lights out. It's usually sloppy, his mop of blond hair and body flopping around, but he plays with such abandon in those last games that it works. It's not perfect or pretty, but it's passionate and, in a way, effortless.

The crowd goes wild, and Conner barely notices because he is having so much fun.

God is after this kind of living from us, and no doubt we are craving it too. But this free, abandoned, passionate kind of life is not possible without one thing. And that one thing is perhaps the most neglected thing in all of modern Christendom.

MYSTERY

Because people mess up in huge, destructive ways, because we are afraid we won't live well without structure, and because it feels like something is missing, we fill gaps with things we think may work: Systems. Rules. Expectations. Prescriptions.

And yet God spent the Old Testament foreshadowing something to come and the New Testament explaining what had come.

> I will put my law in their minds
>> and write it on their hearts.
> I will be their God,
>> and they will be my people. (Jer. 31:33)

Empowered. Convicted. Encouraged. Peaceful. This is the normative pattern of the Spirit of God in a person. Most of us are looking everywhere for a life like this. We are restless because we are exhausted from living in our own strength. We have come to the end of our own striving.

I do not know what you will do when you close this book, but I trust fully in the promise of Scripture that if you commit all your ways to the Lord, he will set your path straight.[2] For me, that has typically looked like knowing only the exact next step in my race and trusting him with the darkness looming ahead.

So together, let's step forward.

THE TAILOR

Spend a few hours alone somewhere quiet where you can
reconnect with God.

Talk to God about

your relationship with him;
your need for him;
the threads that are becoming clear;
the unknowns of your future and purpose.

JOURNAL

In what ways is it difficult for you to trust God?

How have you seen the Holy Spirit lead you in the past?

What are the biggest unknowns burdening you right now?

CHAPTER 18

YOUR THREADS

Friends, you have done a lot of soul searching. You have written about and processed God, his story, and your own story. You've explored your gifts, your scars, and your passions, and hopefully you have paused to pray and had reflective conversations over long meals with friends or family.

Now we are about to pull a lot of this together into one place. And I pray that as you lay out all of the pieces of your life, patterns and passions will surface, connections will be made, and God will more fully be glorified through your threads. He is waiting to weave something beautiful out of them.

Unique design indicates unique purpose. There is not one part of you that exists by accident. God wants to move all of these pieces into epic stories that last forever. After you have laid out all your threads in the chart below, sit across from a few friends and/ or family and hear what they say. Note the connections, have fun dreaming with them, and allow them to dream with you.

Assemble all of the threads of your life here.

INSTRUCTIONS
FOR YOUR

THREADS

---

1. Looking back at the journal pages, narrow your
lists down to the most descriptive words or phrases.

2. Put each list in its place on the following pages.

3. Brainstorm connections and patterns.
Mark up this page. Ask God for discernment as you dream.

4. Lay your threads in front of people who know
you well and can help you dream. (See pages 162–63)

THREADS

GIFTS

_____

_____

_____

_____

_____

ME

GOD'S
STORY

PEOPLE

_____ _____

_____ _____

_____ _____

_____ _____

(YOU NEED) (NEED YOU)

SUFFERING

_____
_____
_____
_____
_____

HOLY
SPIRIT

PASSIONS

_____
_____
_____
_____
_____

PLACES

_____
_____
_____
_____
_____

PURPOSE

DREAM

Gather a dinner with a few friends and lay out the pages with your threads.
First, pray for discernment, and then ask each person these questions:

What connections do you see as you look at my threads?

What ideas do you have for me as I dream about ways God could use all of this?

What do you think is unique about what God has given me?

What could my next steps be?

Where do you sense me holding back?

PART 3

LIVING ON PURPOSE

CHAPTER 19

UNTANGLING A DREAM

Laura and I sat uncomfortably in the very back of the plane, on the row where the seats don't recline. We were flying to Milwaukee, where I would spend two days talking with women about God.

Laura tried to let me have an hour to go over my notes, but she held in her bag a rough version of the threads that you just laid out. They sat there in her bag, yelling for us to study them, to pray over them, to dream with them. Between us we have seven kids, none of whom were present on our plane, so we pulled down our tray tables and had at it.

She stared, sighed, moaned. She saw nothing. It was just her life penciled into some spaces. No big deal; nothing special.

But it blew my mind. Her threads seemed to light up for me. I started circling connections and drawing arrows from some of her gifts to some of her places. She'd never considered the connections that were so obvious to me. I know I wrote the study, but what I saw would have been obvious to anyone. Her gifts were leadership, discernment, strategy. She is passionate about the church reforming to accommodate those who are wounded or doubting. Laura grew up in a world of ministry, but never really knew God's grace. She adopted Aliyah Grace at the same time we adopted Cooper, and from the same Rwandan orphanage. Her heart bends toward Africa. Her reality was that all of her children were about to be school age, and she needed a dream that could provide some income for her family.

My heart raced as I imagined such weighty threads weaving into new stories, new risks. But she couldn't see that she was uniquely built for much of anything. We attach easily to the lie that our lives are average and insignificant.

Part of knowing where you need to be is knowing where you never need to be.

You may be thinking, as you stare and sigh and moan at your threads, that you still do not know what you are supposed to do with your life.

If that is true, and everyone you love has stared at your threads with no answers, let me tell you how to find out and get your answer:

Go do *something*. Anything.

Start somewhere, and through working, building, creating, and leading, you're going to learn things about yourself. I can promise you that if someone is pretty confident about the way they're wired and knows what they want to be doing, it is because they've spent significant time processing and practicing. They have also likely spent a lot of time failing at the wrong endeavors. Part of knowing where you need to be is knowing where you never need to be.

This is a process of discovering. But lean into the process. Because how we spend our lives matters.

THE UNKNOWN COST

I have friends who felt God's call to the mission field and their house sold in two days. And I have friends who felt God's call to the mission field and their house took two years to sell. They lost money, and everything about their lives fell apart in the meantime. Which ones really heard a call from God?

Following God, reading him, is all so beautifully and painfully mysterious. Some of you will clearly see purpose and visions in your threads, and you will run with near certainty that they are callings from God. And some of you will barely detect a hint of a plan and will nervously step out toward a dream; it will feel almost completely dark, but you will do it.

Can God be in both?

I know there may not be complete clarity, but if your heart is willing and you want God's glory, and you give him these pieces of your life, something will happen. He waits for us.

If your heart is willing and you want God's glory, and you give him these pieces of your life, something will happen. He waits for us.

We all doubt and overanalyze, and to some degree, God moves anyway. He moves on with his plans on this earth with or without us. He moves our hearts toward his plans as well. What if we hadn't adopted Cooper? What if we sensed God's call and leading but didn't act? I don't know, but I do know that somehow, despite a lot of resistance from us, God did not let us miss his plans for our lives. Forever I am thankful.

Maybe these small threads are his way of making sure that you don't miss his plans for your life either.

His will eventually will be done on earth as it is in heaven.

LAURA'S THREADS

GIFTS

discernment

attuned to deeper needs

writing

authentic

strategy

ME

GOD'S STORY

PEOPLE

family

close friends

church

neighbors

friends

(YOU NEED)

(NEED YOU)

SUFFERING

invisible – see people – listen

failure – encourage others

hurt from the church – help disillusioned

HOLY SPIRIT

PASSIONS

help others be seen

reform church

creating/transforming with my hands

living for something greater than me

love for the nations/Africa

PLACES

neighborhood

home

work

kids' school

PURPOSE

I grew up thinking that what I said or thought wasn't worth being heard and that it was much easier to be invisible than to know I had value and be ignored. My eyes were always looking inward but at the same time thinking of others who might be hurting like me. It was always my desire to help them. God would begin my transformation and help open my eyes to the value he, as my Creator, gave me. My hurts began to heal. And the desire to help others who felt unseen only grew. My gifts were listening, tuning into others' hurts, empathy, and sometimes discernment. And no matter the circumstance that led others to feel they lacked value, I felt a push to help them be free to know truth—and sometimes God would let me see how he used me. Other times I wasn't so sure. I continued to struggle. My scars were still there.

He has used the hurt in my life to give me *his heart*! He loves the unseen! And he can use me to love them too. I can be a little piece of his heart, maybe just for one. It was clear to me there was an unseen little girl in Rwanda that he wanted to know his love and her value to him. And in bringing her home, God showed me an even bigger piece of the value he places on me.

The day-to-day isn't always as exciting as adopting orphans in Africa. But it's the culmination of God writing his story in the broken pieces of my heart and putting them together to shape his purposes for my life. I am also having fun dreaming about working with a nonprofit in Austin that is reaching the nations through fair trade as a part-time job.

MESSING IT UP

As Laura and I dreamed with her threads in hand, flying over farms and freeways from Texas to Wisconsin, she began to glow. She is my cynical friend, who had persuasively promised this study would not work on her (very encouraging to my ego). She made a swift recovery, saying she thought it might be helpful for others, but she knew herself pretty well and she personally didn't see any magic in it.

But as I circled and connected dots for just a minute, her cynicism began to shift, and she started perking up. For a moment she started to believe that maybe God had more for her, and she hurt for it. She loved raising her kids and she was good at it, but so many other gifts and dreams had lain dormant for years. She was dying for more, but she thought it might be wrong to search for it.

And because she is a very effective skeptical friend, nearly as soon as she lit up, her enthusiasm all began to fade again as she reminded herself and me of her mistakes, her weaknesses, her humanity. I wanted to shake her because it was so expected. She was shutting herself down at the first hint that the "more" she longed for might actually be God's plan for her.

Today she is working toward applying for a role in leadership and strategy with my friend who empowers women around the world through fair trade. Noonday is a company my friend Jessica Honegger built with her God-given threads, empowering women to help care for their families and live their dreams.

Laura also seems to keep finding herself sharing her story with people wounded by the church and questioning their faith. Now she is stepping into conversations with boldness, more confident that these relationships aren't chance encounters.

Reform. Leadership. Strategy. Women. Africa. And a small paycheck.

So before you allow cynicism or defeat to sneak in, listen to God's backward ways. This is the apostle Paul speaking of his weakness:

> But [God] said to me, "My grace is sufficient for you, for my power is made perfect in weakness." Therefore I will boast all the more gladly about my weaknesses, so that Christ's power may rest on me. That is why, for Christ's sake, I delight in weaknesses, in insults, in hardships, in persecutions, in difficulties. For when I am weak, then I am strong. (2 Cor. 12:9–10)

We will not go charge a mountain with our glorious gifts and noble passions. We will do it in our weakness so that God will get the glory.

If you feel lousy when you fill your little chart out because it feels average . . . if you find sin staring back at you next to some great calling . . . if you see the hint of a preposterous dream but think you could never ever fulfill it . . .

Brilliant. Beautiful. That is okay. That is probably exactly right.

The very things I have wished away my entire life seem to be the exact things that keep me close to God.

Do not shrink back. Build your team, dream, and allow them to speak into your life as you speak into theirs. We need kindred warriors to help us divide truth from lies, to speak courage into fear and vision into the fog.

We will do the things God has built for us to do, but it won't be because we are special, great, or powerful. You will do great things because God is moving on this earth to accomplish his purposes for his glory. And just honestly, in my weakness, he looks good. In my usual, normal, averageness, he gets credit.

I'm becoming okay with that, looking a little crazy and ridiculous while he looks awesome.

Please live your purposes. Please lay out your threads and embrace that you exist for specific purposes and no one else can live them like you.

We get to be part of this. It is the highest honor of our lives. Yet it is easy to read books and have moments where that feels true, and then wake up to a sink full of dishes and a job you hate, and forget. There is a war, you know, so before you set down your dream, let's address the most common reasons we hold back.

CHAPTER 20

SHRINKING BACK

Zac and I sat at dinner with some friends, asking them terribly intrusive questions. We want to know people's souls and have an awkward way with small talk, so we skip it. Zac asked, "What gets you excited right now?"

Immediately, Rebecca's eyes sparked, and without giving it thought, she let her words bleed about a need she saw in the American church. She had a big vision of how the need could be met. Then suddenly her eyes dropped, almost regretting what she had just revealed. She was unsure of herself and yet busting out of her skin to do something about the need she saw. She quickly pushed her passion safely and neatly back inside herself.

This was becoming a theme around me. Since signing on to write my first book, I had become a type of priest for friends' confessions of unfulfilled passions, as if watching me be brave convicted them. Nope—I should clarify. They weren't seeing me be brave; they were actually seeing me be afraid but obey anyway. And somehow witnessing the mess of that process woke them up a little, made them uncomfortable, and made them wonder what it was they were supposed to be doing and why it was they weren't doing it.

As we were getting ready for bed after that dinner, Zac casually said, "Men are often confused about what they are supposed to do. It seems more women know deep down—they are just afraid to do it."

Something is stopping us from running wild toward our purposes. What caused the shift in Rebecca's eyes? For a moment she felt free—unconcerned with any perceptions and opinions while she danced around an idea that contained her passion and imagination and heart.

Then something shifted, reminding her that in some way she shouldn't go there. She stopped herself.

Why?

Because there is a war. And I wish I were being dramatic. But it's real, and you know it because you feel it too. It's a resistance that comes any time you consider doing something potentially important, and suddenly all you want to do is grab a bowl of peanut M&M's and get lost in your third viewing of *Downton Abbey*. In *The War of Art*, Steven Pressfield observed, "The more important the work, the more resistance you need to expect to feel."[1]

Why does it feel so hard to *not* be numb? Because there is a war waging for our hearts, to shut them down. To disable those who love Jesus, and especially those who are surrendered.

So I propose *we fight*.

The writer of Hebrews was addressing Hebrew believers who had tasted fear. They were exhausted, their friends and family had been imprisoned or killed, and they were wondering if living for

Jesus was worth it. They were scared for their lives and families. They were weary.

"In just a little while, he who is coming will come and will not delay. . . . But my righteous one will live by faith. And I take no pleasure in the one who *shrinks back*" (Heb. 10:37–38, emphasis added). Let those words haunt you. I shrink back a lot, and it haunts me too. We all are plagued with inner wars:

"I shrink back because I'm afraid."
"I don't trust myself."
"I'm confused because I'm not exactly sure what it is he wants me to do."
"I don't know for sure that I can do what God wants me to do."
"I've already got too much to do right in front of me."

I don't know what it is for you, but I bet that in some way, in some place in your soul, you are shrinking back. Even though we were saved and have God with us to live our callings, we all are shrinking back. So let's go there. *Why* are you shrinking back? *Why* are you afraid to live your calling? Where do you feel the most resistance?

PHYSICALLY?

"I don't have enough margin in this season of life."
"I am already strapped financially."
"I can't neglect other responsibilities."
"It's really not a big deal."
"I'm too young or old."
"I am not 100 percent sure this is God's will."
"It's not going to make a difference."

EMOTIONALLY?

"It feels lonely."

"I crave security."

"I can't control what is going to happen."

"I am scared I'll fail."

"I am not a leader."

"I am screwed up."

"I want a comfortable life."

RELATIONALLY?

"My spouse will not support this."

"What if God takes someone I love?"

"I'll look foolish."

"If I do this, I will let people down."

"My family doesn't understand."

"People think I'm crazy."

"My life will look different than my friends'."

SPIRITUALLY?

"I am not good enough for God to use me."

"I can't even pray right now."

"I don't know if I trust God's plan for me."

"Do I really believe God is real?"

"I am stuck in sin."

"I don't think God even sees me."

"Is it worth it?"

"What if God doesn't show up?"

"What if I am misreading God?"

So do the work. Ask yourself, why are you shrinking back?

FIGHT FEAR

I shrink back because I'm afraid. I am afraid of what I will lose. What if following God costs me the things I love most? What if he takes my spouse or child? What if I lose approval or comfort or success or control? What if I give my life, and he takes away the deepest desires of my heart?

In God's beautiful irony, as I write about fear today, I just pulled the trigger on one of the scariest callings of my life, a vision that has haunted me for over seven years. It is an embarrassingly large, preposterous vision. Only someone stupid or possessed by God would dare to dream of what we are about to do.

And sitting on an old red couch decorated with little brown horses at my sister's ranch, sending texts revealing our crazy plans, I find myself in that frantic moment with the ground inching closer and the pull-string on the chute not working. I'm just stuck in the silent wait.

I am terrified. This could fail. This may not even be from God. And I am going to do it anyway.

Welcome to my brain. Fear lives in me, and I can't seem to make it go away. Everything in me wants me to shrink back even on the good days, and especially on the bad ones.

And oh, how I wish I were writing this years from now, when this dream's existence was sure. Fear pushes its way to the table. I am hosting it and feeding it and offering it coffee as I write about how ridiculous it is to be afraid when God is for us. But here is the thing:

I am terrified. This could fail. This may not even be from God. And I am going to do it anyway.

We have to deal with fear because it is possible that it will make us miss the best parts of life.

We all face fear. But we must kill fear like it is the devil, because it usually is. We do not belong to the one who shrinks back; we belong to the one who moved through his blood and sweat and despair and fear and reluctance in the garden of Gethsemane and said, "Not my will, but yours be done. I belong to you and I will live for you and die for you."[2] He walked headfirst into his death. So fight with me.

FIGHT UNCERTAINTY

I shrink back because I'm unclear. Honestly, I have never known anything for 100 percent sure. God's will usually is revealed for certain after something happens. Were we 100 percent sure we were supposed to adopt Cooper? No. We just had a burden we couldn't shake, and at some point when that burden lines up with Scripture, you have to ask yourself, "Is this God?"

You won't believe how much you actually *do* know. And we have a thick book from God about who he is and what he wants for us that we can absolutely trust. But honestly, there is a lot we know about ourselves. He likes his kids completely hanging on to him for dear life more than he cares about the perfect plan being executed. He is after *us*, and uncertainty is usually what keeps us glued to his side.

He is in the trenches with us. In the fear. In the uncertainty. He is in the unknown—knowing and leading and working. What we don't know yet is meant to lead us to dependence.

FIGHT DISTRACTION

I shrink back because I'm distracted. I've already got too much to do right in front of me. We have to be the most distractible generation on earth. There is just so much out there fighting for our attention.

I have four kids, church, friends, and dry cleaning, and everybody around me seems to need to eat all the time. I have a pretty full-time job in ministry, and on and on like everyone else. But somehow I still manage to watch every season of *Friday Night Lights* and *30 Rock*, use Facebook to keep up with people I haven't seen in fifteen years, and take a lot of baths and a few naps. And there is nothing *wrong* with any of it—the things I have to do, and the things I want to do, and the things I just need so my soul doesn't shrivel up. *But* if I do all of it and never consider that there is a bigger reason I am here, I could be missing the point—missing the Only thing for all the small things.

> There is an art to living that is far above the base human instinct of survival. I want to live beautifully.

All things are permissible but not all things are beneficial.[3] There is an art to living that is far above the base human instinct of survival. I want to live beautifully. I want to live like my good friend Julie, who has died twice and been resuscitated, and who can't do small talk because she knows she may cross over to heaven any minute. She just doesn't have the stomach for chitchat. She manages to do her dishes and tuck her kids in and see patients in her job. But she lives more beautifully and intentionally than anyone I know. She lives slowly and breathes every moment in. She sits on her deck as her boys wrestle and chase balls. She sips wine and asks questions that move us all to wonder aloud about things that matter. Let's make that kind of beautiful life. Without wasting a minute.

FIGHT INSECURITY

I shrink back because I'm insecure. Every single time I stand up in front of ten people or ten thousand, I tremble. I shake. I have a very physical reminder of my insecurity. And I've learned to not wish it away. My insecurity makes me pray every time. When I get on my knees, God reminds me that this is about him and not me. He reminds me that I have nothing to prove anymore.

Because of grace we have nothing to prove. Our confidence is in the security and power God gives us, not in ourselves. To know that you are absolutely treasured, unconditionally, changes you in this way. You feel free, and you want to run with a God who would love you like that. To know that we do not measure up and that we don't have to because of Jesus, because of grace, means that life gets a whole lot more fun.

FIGHT COMPARISON

It is nearly impossible to do anything with our threads while we are looking side to side. One of my most creative friends called me recently, as burdened as I had ever heard her. She held a dream and couldn't seem to start it because someone she barely knew was doing something similar already. Rather than listening to God alone, we look around and compare and allow our inadequacies to consume us. Then it's over before it starts.

> Together, if we could cheer for each other instead of criticize, and obey instead of compare, and fear God instead of being paralyzed with fear of men, we could watch God just flat show off in front of us.

We want a revolution, but most of us wish someone else would start it. We're embarrassingly cynical and we shoot leaders down for sport, so no wonder we're all afraid to lead! Instead, let's help each other fight our fears rather than taking each other down. We must focus on our races and cheer others toward theirs.

Together, if we could cheer for each other instead of criticize, and obey instead of compare, and fear God instead of being paralyzed with fear of men, we could watch God just flat show off in front of us.

We need each other, and we are killing each other. In Hebrews 12, the writer pleads with those who are shrinking back:

Since we are surrounded by such a great cloud of witnesses . . . (v. 1)

We have each other.

Let us throw off everything that hinders and the sin that so easily entangles . . . (v. 1)

Because we are free.

And let us run with perseverance the race marked out for us . . . (v. 1)

We have a marked race—each of us. We can't miss it for fear.

Fixing our eyes on Jesus, the pioneer and perfecter of faith. For the joy set before him he endured the cross, scorning its shame, and sat down at the right hand of the throne of God . . . so that you will not grow weary and lose heart. (vv. 2–3)

We fall apart when we look at our fears and inadequacies and compare ourselves to every other runner. But fix your eyes on a God like Jesus, and you will not quit. You will not shrink back. Not from others, and not from yourself.

Risk something. Step out and fail. Be the fool. Build a life that needs our God.

CHAPTER 21

WHEN WOMEN DREAM

Meredith was a new friend; our daughters had become friends at school. We sat together outside at a park as our girls tenderly mothered their dolls. We four must have looked so perfectly ideal. The two of us in our flip flops with coffee and a Diet Coke, talking about end-of-school activities with our two girls obediently playing with their appropriate toys sweetly together. Even their dolls' hair was looking pretty good that day.

But if there is one thing I am not, it is perfectly, sweetly appropriate. Rarely. Ever.

Like those of nearly every other human I know, Meredith's eyes were heavy. If I were to guess from the look of them, it seemed as if her soul was all boxed in. And with my impatience for small talk, I began intruding fairly quickly.

Initially she darted around my questions about her own personal hopes and dreams with a story about a good friend who had become distant. This friend had made some pretty brave and intentional changes in her life; the friend and her husband were dreaming, and some of their dreams had led them far from the norms their small church community had come to most value. They weren't in sin; in fact their dreams sounded incredibly unselfish and risky. But some of their dreams had failed, and some of their former friends had confronted their new ventures as if they were sinful. Meredith's angst over this friend was palpable.

Why had she brought up her friend, when my question was, "What are you dreaming about?" She had watched a friend take a risk and be judged for it. The friend was criticized, and then some of those dreams even failed.

My question felt threatening to Meredith because she was keenly aware of the "rules" to being a respected woman in her small world. The rules were:

1. Stay home full-time with the kids.
2. Don't pursue your own passions and dreams and take risks; it's selfish.
3. Volunteer as a homeroom mom.
4. Don't miss a game for any of the five sports each of your four kids plays, or a party or a field trip.
5. Dinner should be worthy of a Pinterest pinning and should be on the table by 6:00 every night.

Now, obviously, some of the most powerful ministry on this earth is happening through stay-at-home moms and homeroom moms and at Pinterest-worthy dinners at 6:00. These things are noble and not the problem. Certainly, these tasks and thousands of others have to get done in homes, schools, and offices, whether we feel passionate about them or not. The problem is not in these roles or duties themselves; the problem is when these things turn into man-made rules *mandatory* for godly women.

Being a great mother and serving at the school weren't strangling Meredith. Feeling like she couldn't do anything out of this acceptable box was what was strangling her soul, her dreams, and her obedience to God.

Her particular situation occurred in the South in a conservative church, but I have another friend who lives in New York City, and she feels judged that she *doesn't* work outside her home and has chosen to homeschool her kids, even though these are her personal convictions and callings. And I have another friend who has felt judged for choosing to adopt a child as a single woman. And another friend who is drowning in toddlerhood and feels judged for not having the capacity to do one other thing than be sure her kids stay alive.

This is happening in a million forms in a million places. The rules seem to change in each church, each city, each country, even throughout history in each generation. Unique versions of handbooks describing "how to be a godly woman" seem to exist wherever I go.

Women, we are so dang hard on each other. We have to stop.

Women, we are so dang hard on each other. We have to stop.

We are in the midst of a generation laced with social and gender pressures. The weight of "the rules" for women in the church, home, and workplace is so heavy, I think we forget how all the different pressures are carried into nearly every choice we make, nearly every dream we dream.

If we are all obeying God with our unique gifts and visions, our dreaming, our obedience, then our roles should look beautifully diverse. We each look unique on the outside, and I assure you we are even more intricately designed on the inside.

What are some of the tensions you feel as a woman?

Here are some examples:

- "My husband feels threatened when I dream."
- "I feel like I am wasting an expensive education, but I feel called to stay at home to raise my kids."
- "My gifts are so strong that I am worried if I really succeed as a strong woman, no man will want to marry me."
- "My kids are going to be wounded if I can't be present at everything for them."
- "People don't like strong women."
- "My husband has so many expectations of my role at home that there is no way I could do anything outside of that."
- "I want to go overseas, but I feel like I need to wait until I get married."
- "I have to provide for my kids as a single mom; there is no one else. Dreaming is not a luxury I can afford."
- "I have gifts of teaching or leadership that my church doesn't encourage women to use."
- "My elderly parents need me or my grandkids need me. This isn't my dream, but this is my reality and it is all I have time for."
- "I feel called to adopt and my husband doesn't."
- "I can't do it all."

So what do we do?

As God called me into a more public and demanding ministry, I saw the writing on the wall: Some games were going to be missed. Sitters would become part of my family. My husband might be overshadowed by my calling at times. I would have to travel. My strong gifts would hit many ceilings within the church. I was turning in the title I had proudly worn for more than a decade: stay-at-home mom.

So many tensions lay on top of my calling because of my gender. I spent a bit of time wishing away my gender, but since that wasn't happening, I found myself wishing away my calling.

One memory specifically haunted me. I remembered being home from college and sitting in church with my parents. Our pastor preached that morning on biblical motherhood. One of the women in our church led a very influential international ministry. In the midst of his sermon he asked her to come to the stage, where he announced that she was quitting her ministry to stay at home with her kids.

The church erupted into a standing ovation.

In my head, the applause turned to boos and condemnation as I saw myself moving in the exact opposite direction of the woman my church celebrated many years ago. Even though there wasn't a doubt in my mind I was moving in obedience to God, I feared appearing like I was in sin because my calling didn't fit the prescribed picture of motherhood in my conservative community.

That woman was almost certainly obeying God that day in her unique calling, just as I was struggling to obey. And the church was likely applauding her obedience. But all of our views of our roles are shaped by our culture and by approving or disapproving messages.

OBEY GOD

The clearest way to obey God is through studying and applying his Word. But "obey Scripture" . . . I wish it were simple. Nearly every respected teacher and theologian defines the roles of women from Scripture differently.

I will do my best to obey God within the boundaries and

freedom Scripture gives me as a woman. But the roles of women are sometimes hard to determine in Scripture, so we should build our convictions and then give grace in the gray spaces. Personal convictions cannot become law.

We must separate biblical mandates from cultural Christian values.

TRUST GOD WITH THE COST

I felt physically burdened from worry that my kids would suffer because of God's calling on my life. And if I am honest, they have. This calling wasn't just on my life; it would go on to cost something from my entire family. Every calling has a cost.

As women, we often foresee the cost to ourselves and the people we love, and we stop.

We must separate biblical mandates from cultural Christian values.

But because God was building this dream, the very costs I most feared for my children have birthed the most character. One night as I lay in a Holiday Inn Express in Milwaukee after speaking to many women about God, my thirteen-year-old son Conner relived over the phone the game I had so painfully missed that day. I was feeling the cost; he was feeling the cost. I was just so sad.

At the end of the call he said, "Mom, we prayed for the women you spoke to today. How did it go?"

And then Cooper, my Rwandan five-year-old, took the phone and yelled, "Mama, are you telling people about Jesus?"

My heart melted because the costs I feared were building deeper compassion for the mission of God and the needs of others in my people.

You may think your calling isn't as spiritual. Your cost may be a financial sacrifice because you are leaving your job, or maybe you are lying in your Holiday Inn room telling your kids about a sales conference. But whatever the calling and whoever it is costing, the point is we are all living out the purposes of God for his glory here, in unique places with unique demands. And God calculates the costs of our callings. We don't need to be afraid of the price we'll pay; we just need to weigh it and not forfeit our God-given responsibilities for selfish gain.

I've realized my kids didn't need me at every game. They need parents who fear and obey God first. But if they saw me neglecting them out of vain ambition . . . kids are smart; I imagine they would be wounded right now. We are a family on mission together, supporting each other, sacrificing for each other, and building the name of God here in our own ways. I want my kids to be brave and willing to obey, even if that means sacrifice. I have to model that first.

CHOOSE FEWER VOICES

Our heads get so crowded. There are opinions shouting out everywhere, from parents, pastors, spouses, friends, and coworkers. If we let them all decide who we are and what we will do with our lives, it gets way too crowded.

We feel so confused and wonder why we can't hear God. The thing is, we have to decide who we will listen to. So when I dream or sense some direction, I take that to my people.

Pick your voices and then be prepared and willing to disappoint the rest.

Scripture. The Holy Spirit. My husband. My elders and mentor. My small group of friends who love God deeply and aren't afraid to kick me in the tail or push me to obey, even if my obedience looks different from theirs. To these voices I submit; I receive truth and I count the cost.

Pick your voices and then be prepared and willing to disappoint the rest. We have to decide whom we will listen to and whom we won't. You are not obligated to bend to the convictions and judgment of every person around you, or you will never do anything. Choose to obligate yourself to a few trusted voices.

When my few voices affirm and release me, I run. And when they pull me in, I stop and listen.

A DREAM-RELEASING SPOUSE

The main earthly voice in my life is my husband. I often am asked, "As a mother and pastor's wife and writer . . . how do you do it all?" I have a lot of help: sitters and help with cleaning and administrative help. But the most obvious answer is that without the blessing, leadership, and sacrifice of my husband, with all I have in my life, I would be unable to do any of it. We have fought our way to a good marriage, and it has not been easy. But as passionate and strong and independent as I can be, it actually feels so good to come under his leadership.

There isn't a doubt that the measure of support we feel from our husbands, if we are married, will and should affect our dreams.

I asked Zac to share his road to releasing and leading me to use my gifts and fulfill my callings. So wives, hand this over to your husbands.

A LETTER FROM ZAC

It was a perfect, eighty-degree day on the lawn of a plantation house in downtown Little Rock. This was the day all of our dreams would become a reality. I stood looking in Jennie's eyes, and before God, I promised to lead her by daily dying to my selfish desires, just as Christ did. The record states that the pastor read that day from Ephesians 5:28 to 30, "Husbands ought to love their wives as their own bodies . . . for no one ever hated their own body, but they feed and care for it, just as Christ does the church, for we are members of his body."

But honestly, I don't remember the ceremony very well or the charge of the pastor, or the vows I spoke to Jennie. I just know in the midst of sixteen years of marriage, many moves, four kids, mortgages, and unfulfilling jobs, the dreams we dreamed on many dates before marriage quickly gave way to a lot of weighty responsibility.

I went from trying to win this girl's heart and longing for her freedom to pursue God's dreams for her, to actually using the Bible's language of submission to kill any dream that would inconvenience or threaten me. So, not long after the wedding day, Jennie found herself with a passive-aggressive, emotionless husband, and her God-given passions and dreams began to die.

At the time, I thought I was right and biblically justified in my "leadership" of Jennie. But I was wrong. I had memorized "Wives, submit yourselves to your own husbands," but had no clue of what it meant for husbands to *nourish and cherish* their wives (Eph. 5:22).

Honestly, it took years for me to grow in maturity to see my error. And if you find yourself reading this and realizing you no longer have a clue how to nourish and cherish, take courage; neither do countless other men reading this book that their wives asked them to read. So hang with me through the next few pages because I want to help you lead your wives. My goal is not to beat you down, but rather to call you to one of the most noble callings of your life.

Husbands, to *nourish and cherish* your wife means to unleash your wife to be everything she has been designed to be in Christ. Yes, that means you are to live with her in an understanding way: to know the hurts she brings into marriage, to know her passions, and to listen to her dreams, even when you have no clue what to do with them. To nourish and to cherish means you become the most powerful earthly display of unconditional love. And part of that unconditional love is shown as she gives herself to the many seemingly mediocre tasks of daily life. But husbands, don't miss this: to nourish and cherish *also* means taking the initiative to shepherd her gifts and callings and to help her dream.

So how did I miss all that? Why did the dreaming die so quickly after "I do"?

I think I can boil down my failures to nourish and cherish to two reasons:

1. I had a darkened, jaded view of submission. I used submission to squelch my wife so I could justify my "more important" pursuits. Of course few of us would say that as men, our callings and gifts and passions are more important than those of our wives. But that is often how I led. So tonight, or on a date this week, ask your wife if she feels safe to dream with you. Ask her if she feels cherished and empowered to use her gifts.

2. I was insecure in who I was in Christ. If I was not performing well at work or if I didn't have a fulfilling job, I felt like a failure. My worth was not coming from the approval of the God of the universe, but from the disapproval I felt internally. Here is what I know to be true: an insecure husband will never be able to cheer for his wife's callings

or cherish and nourish her gifts. Insecure husbands think about themselves first. There were countless times early in my marriage when I would secretly resent my wife's gifts. Or maybe I would even be so noble to encourage her to use her gift of teaching, only to resent being left with the kids as she went to use those gifts.

It took me years to realize the problem wasn't being married to a passionate, gifted, "unsubmissive" wife who would start using her gifts only to have me reel her back into reality. The problem was me: my misunderstanding of my role to lead us as a team on mission, and my resentment of seeing my wife walking in freedom while I was immersed in my own insecurities.

So, husbands, if you are still reading this, I believe you really want your wife to be all she is designed to be in Christ. You want your children to see a mom serving and using her gifts in and outside your home. And I believe you want to want to sit across from your wife on that date and affirm her God-given dreams and callings.

So, how do you become a dream-releasing husband?

- **Realize you have nothing to prove.** As long as you are searching to prove yourself or your identity, you will never grasp how completely loved and fully accepted you are before God. If you are in Christ, you have nothing left to prove. Jesus fulfilled your desperate desire to measure up. The more that truth sinks in, the less you will look to your job or money or your wife for fulfillment. Dream-releasing husbands are secure in Christ.

- **Take hold of your role.** Realize that your call to *nourish and cherish* your wife does not depend on her performance. Christ gave his life for the very people (you and me) who put him on the cross. As you become more secure in your own identity in Christ, you will begin to experience the joy of seeing your wife use her gifts and respond to her callings.
- **Embrace the loss of control.** As you become more secure in Christ and begin cheering on your wife to use her gifts too, you will feel a new tension surface: a life that feels semi-chaotic. You realize that what you had been calling "balance" for your family was really a determined effort to control your life at all costs. You see, God never promises balance. So this new life that feels semi-chaotic is likely a symptom of a couple attempting to follow the leading of the Holy Spirit. And no matter the suffering or sacrifice or a sink full of dirty dishes or lack of clean boxers, you will be full of joy because Jesus is infinitely more satisfying than the god of control.

Men, husbands, this is God's call on our lives. It is one of the noblest callings on the planet. And I'll bet, in the midst of your leading courageously, you will rediscover the woman you fell in love with.

—Zac

Women, as you read, know that there were many years when I did not feel released to use my gifts. And in my insecurity, I fought for my rights and nagged for my freedom. That didn't work. Our marriage became healthy again with a lot of time and prayer and counseling and surrender. We are having a lot of fun these days. It is worth the work.

Scripture talks about a day when there will no longer be slave or free, Jew or Greek, male or female.[1] But that day hasn't come yet. These tensions won't last forever. My little girl really will be an incredible mother if those dolls turn into real babies. But as a woman I pray that her worth and identity aren't based on how she performs roles as a mother, or a daughter, or a wife, or a friend, or an employee. I pray that her soul is steadied and secure because her eyes are laser-focused on the one who built and rescued her soul.

CHAPTER 22

FOCUSED AND STEADY

It was the middle of the night. I lay on the same sofa with the horses on it at my sister's ranch and stared at a new ceiling. Six or seven years had passed, and a few more kids pushed time to move faster than in the early days with only one newborn. I lay there, eyes wide, sensing a calling I would have never been brave enough to make up. It was rare because it was so clear. And yet all the pieces and threads of my life were chaotically still flying around in my head—no clarity, no order. I'd sorted through some of the threads, but I still had no idea what to do with them. And now I held a nearly ridiculous new dream:

Gather and equip your generation.

Only someone stupid or possessed by God would even consider that such a call was not pretend. I wasn't sure it was God, so I pushed it away for years. I had no means of doing such a preposterous thing—gathering a generation. It was ridiculous. I should clarify: I didn't grow up charismatic enough. I didn't live expecting visions from God.

I was busy living out a huge calling already: motherhood. I held no connections and no aspirations to build a platform or even write a book. Years passed, and I don't remember even thinking much about that night.

And now, after more than half a decade, I somehow find myself with so many people and threads in place, I actually consider that perhaps the whisper was from God. So on that sofa that night, with painful fear, God and I launched a vision to reach a generation. I expect it will take a while, and I expect to not quite get to every person on earth in our generation. But here goes.

I wish the threads were more perfectly untangled. I'm in process and doing my best to listen to God's Spirit and respond in obedience, despite the insanity of it all. Thank God that he builds his plans on this earth in spite of us.

At nearly the same time, my football-coach-turned-pastor husband, who loves to start things and has spent the last fifteen years of his life in vocational ministry, was feeling his threads and God's Spirit rerouting him to the marketplace. He dreamed with his best friend about using business as ministry, and what it would look like to launch businesses as they invest deeply into the lives of the men they are working beside.

As I was being called deeper into vocational ministry, Zac was being called out into ministry through business. God's stories may lead to getting paid as a pastor or as a clerk at a clothing shop, raising children or teaching them math, displaying him through excellence as a writer of news or theology. He is creative like that, God is.

So what now?

What if you live like this?

What if you run?

What if you dream God's dreams?

What if you obey in your unique, beautiful spot here?

Austin's city slogan is "Keep Austin Weird." And Austin loves races. Nearly everyone who lives here has run a race. We have races where people throw paint at you and races that drag you through obstacle courses. There is one weird race in Austin called "Run for Your Lives." It's a zombie race. People dressed up like zombies chase you and try to attack you while you run.

I haven't run in it, but I can promise you I would get a decent time in that race. I would book it if zombies were chasing me. So would you.

And in similar odd fashion, I expect if you are running your race, whatever it is, the enemy is on your tail. Even if you are on a more defined, marked path, this race is long. This race is hard.

As Zac and I were both headed into our newest places to meet need, Sarah had her strokes. A dark, terrifying despair found its way to my soul. I've never felt such a physical weight pushing me down, so I daydreamed about quitting my race—playing it over and over in my head, justifying it over and over.

I still loved God.

But I did not want to keep running. I wanted to be comfortable more than I wanted God's will for my days.

Simultaneously, our children led us to the emergency room four times in two months. One trip was life threatening and one was brain threatening, and one may still be a chronic illness. My grandmother was placed in hospice and was processing death with my mother, while my best friend lay upstairs on another floor of the hospital in her room, unable to move, unable to talk.

You know how life goes like that sometimes.

Was it a spiritual attack?

I don't know. It did feel like zombies were on our tail. I will say if it is you, Devil, *it is below the belt to mess with my kids.*

What I do know: there is a very real and very active battle, and the prize is faith. God gives faith and Satan steals faith. God loves faith more than any other thing in us, and Satan hates our faith more than any other thing.

Faith is the measure to which we believe God is God. And faith is the measure to which we let God be God.

Faith is the measure to which we believe God is God. And faith is the measure to which we let God be God.

We were living a little more bravely and obediently, and it felt like something or someone was threatened by it. By this journey, this project. It turns out, this is a marathon—not for faint souls and not for those seeking easy and happy quickly. And as I wanted to quit, my people reminded me of my God. We need our people. And needs, like Gotham for Batman, whispered to me to not stop. Sarah, who had always told me I couldn't quit, couldn't let me off the hook now.

Zac, of course, still follows football like any good Texas boy, and he passed me the story of Chip Kelly, the Oregon Ducks football coach. Coach Kelly has a saying that has almost become the slogan of the entire state. And I suggest we make it ours too: "Win the day."

"WIN THE DAY"

Don't dream of winning Super Bowls or even Saturday's game on Monday morning. Win practice that day, in that moment. Win that day, whatever it holds.

Will our little tribe of missionaries (that we hope you will join) reach a generation? I don't know.

But today, I'll spend a few moments alone with God and really talk to him. And I'll write you these words and send a few e-mails and hop on a few seemingly insignificant calls and read *Miss Fannie's Hats* to my children. I'll sweep the cereal crumbs up from breakfast and cheer for my husband as he takes some financial risks to follow God. Even though I'm scared and kind of want to say, "Heck no." Even though every piece of today feels small.

I'll do today, glancing up and remembering a race is completed the same way this book is completed. Step by step. Word by word. Day by day.

Bill Gates said, "People often overestimate what will happen in the next two years and underestimate what will happen in ten."[1] Don't underestimate obedience over a long time.

Great people don't do great things. God does great things with surrendered people. And surrender happens every day in one thousand small moments.

Joseph swept his floors, sat on his prison floor, made strategies for farmers, built storehouses, and dreamed dreams. And somehow, he died having saved many lives and honoring God in his generation.

Great people don't do great things. God does great things with surrendered people. And surrender happens every day in one thousand small moments.

Win the day. Run the steps in front of you today.

CHAPTER 23

THE END OF
MUNDANE

I took Caroline, my seven-year-old, to school late this morning. I don't know why; she was tired and cuddly and I like having her around. My day's agenda was to write these final words to you. It's time to be finished and to let you go about running your races. But I'd been stumbling around these words for days (okay, weeks), and it felt as if God had not issued them yet.

As I walked into the school to check-in Caroline, late with no real excuse except "she needed me," I saw one of the administrators of our school, Brenda. She came a bit out of her way to hug me, which surprised me, and then she whispered, "I feel like I am supposed to tell you something."

I kissed my Caroline good-bye, right on the lips. She rolled her eyes and giggled and skipped off, soul full of slow time together.

Brenda held me close as we walked out to a bench together. We'd bonded years ago when my oldest son was the primary troublemaker of fifth grade (yep), and we'd cried and wondered and prayed that a hardness would crumble in him. You bond with people who cry over your rebel children with you.

This morning her eyes filled with tears again as this lovely, Spirit-filled mother, teacher, and fifty-year-old rock of a woman tenderly shared that months earlier she had been arrested and charged with a felony. A loaded handgun was found in her carry-on bag at the airport, as she and her son were flying to visit a college together. The loaded gun was tucked inside a bag that she had taken from her father's house when he passed away; she was unaware of its presence.

But in moments, she went from a college visit to being tackled and handcuffed as a terrorist in the airport. Because the charges were so severe, she was sent to federal prison; she had her ankles shackled. She couldn't find an attorney to represent her at first because of the crime's magnitude.

The charges were eventually dropped, and her life fully restored. However, today, months later, she's pulling me down on a bench with tears and urgency to share this with me. Why?

Because in the twenty-four hours she was in prison, in her shackles, she glimpsed the eyes of women starving for God. Prison starves for God, and God took her pure little light right to the darkness. One prisoner had grabbed Brenda by the arm and said, "You glow. Why do you glow?"

I wrapped Brenda in my arms, unsure she would let me tell her story here (she did), but completely sure God was giving me his parting words for you.

We've done important work together, and you may find yourself today in gym shorts and a T-shirt or work clothes and not in ankle shackles, but hear me: you live in a world that is dark and craving light. People's eyes are starving for God, dying for freedom.

Your view of your life may be small, but nothing about your life is small.

Every moment is granted for purposes we can't see. Every breath is issued for eternal things left undone. We brush against people in check-out lines who will live forever in heaven or hell, and we contain God. Try to tell me your life is insignificant. Try to tell me that anything about this life is insignificant.

Your view of your life may be small, but nothing about your life is small.

Feel the weight of the calling you have received, but not so you feel guilt. So that you feel great worth in your soul and in the work of your day.

After leaving Brenda, as I drove here to my coffee-shop office where many of these words have bled onto these pages, a friend told me that the previous night some friends asked their waiter at Olive Garden if there was anything he needed prayer for, and he began to weep.

The waiter's best friend had just been killed in a car wreck. Outside of Olive Garden that night, Henry prayed to receive Christ, as these friends ran to a bookstore and had his first Bible engraved with his name.

THE WEIGHT OF GLORY

We are souls undone and rebuilt by the Spirit of God. As God surveys this earth, he sees light and darkness. And he sees *his* light, his Spirit wandering through neighborhoods, offices, schools, Wal-marts, Chick-fil-A playgrounds, and eating breadsticks at Olive Gardens. We possess God and are filled with him for the very same purposes that Peter, John, Paul, Mary, and Luke in the early church were filled with him. We are filled with God to pour him into the darkness, pour him into the broken souls who are starving for something.

There are no average, small dreams, and no average people. There are no meaningless moments as we go to the gym or cook macaroni or handle shipping orders gone wrong or nurse our babies. If we were sitting across from each other and you pleaded with me—*begged* me—to believe you were average, your life was boring, there was nothing significant to anything you were doing, you could not convince me. You could not.

There are moments of cuddling and skipping school and public kisses on the lips that embarrass our children, who need full souls to be light to their world. There are moments with jumpsuits in prison cells, metaphorical or real, that exist for others' freedom. There are moments with new Bibles outside Olive Garden. There are moments with tangled threads over dinners where simple visions are affirmed and neighborhood boot camps are born. There are moments in speech therapy offices when you hug a mother who is fighting back tears because she wonders if her autistic toddler will get to go to mainstream kindergarten. There are many moments of sweeping up crumbs from breakfast that no one sees and couldn't possibly matter, except that as order is brought from chaos, your family flourishes a little more that day.

There are moments in offices, when you swallow all pride as coworkers gossip and misrepresent you to others, and God draws near in the very moment you have never felt so alone. There are moments in hospital waiting rooms when the world turns upside down, when you can shake your fist and fall down. In the darkest moments, God was building the very brightest ones.

Do you feel restless?

There is more. A story too weighty and beautiful to bear. A story stretched out beyond ten million years from today.

Brenda told me on the bench this morning that days before her arrest, she had just finished the book *The Weight of Glory* by C. S. Lewis. As the words of this title fell out of her mouth, they so perfectly captured the reason these closing words had felt so impossible to write.

I feel a weight of glory.

An indescribable burden.

A holy, God-given passion burning in my soul for you, for us, for our time here. Because I know we will blink and be together with God forever, and there is life to be lived here.

Lewis said, "To please God . . . to be a real ingredient in the divine happiness . . . to be loved by God, not merely pitied, but delighted in as an artist delights in his work or a father in a son—it seems impossible, a weight or burden of glory which our thoughts can hardly sustain. But so it is."[1]

So it is. We are

- built by God;
- rescued by God;
- filled with God;
- pleasing to God.

May we never get over it. This weight of glory we carry is the promise of more, the promise of kingdoms coming that our imaginations can't contain.

So don't waste your days any longer, staring at ceilings, wondering if there is more.

There is more. Take the threads of your life and go live like it.

HOW TO FIND GOD

I can't imagine a more restless feeling than being unsure about the meaning of life and the future of my soul. As long as we are on this earth, we will ache for something bigger, because we were designed for something bigger—something better. We are designed for an intimate relationship with God forever.

Saint Augustine said, "You have made us for Yourself, and our hearts are restless until they find their rest in You."[1]

We had a perfect relationship with God until sin entered the world through Adam and Eve. And with sin came the promise of death and eternal separation from God. But from the moment of the first sin, God issued a promise that would bring us back to him.

The penalty had to be paid.

Our sin was to be placed on a perfect sacrifice. God would send his own blameless, perfect Son to bear our sin and suffer our fate—to get us back.

Jesus came fulfilling thousands of years of prophecy, lived a perfect life, and died a gruesome death, reconciling our payment for our sin. Then after three days, he defeated death, rose from the grave, and now is seated with the Father, waiting for us.

Anyone who accepts the blood of Jesus for the forgiveness of their sin is adopted as a child of God and issued God's very own Spirit to seal and empower us to live this life for him.

Our souls are restless until they rest in God. We were made for him, and he gave everything so that our souls could finally and forever rest in him.

If you have never trusted Christ for the forgiveness of your sins, you can do that this moment. Just tell him your need for him and tell him of your trust in him as your Lord and Savior.

LEAVING BEHIND
&
MOVING FORWARD

Sometimes it's helpful to see where we've been and where we're going, just to get perspective. I have found this to be helpful in my work with groups.

What are you leaving behind?
And what are you moving toward?

I am leaving behind

_____

I am moving toward

_____

The stories and examples of others
who have been through this project . . .

I am leaving behind

I am moving toward

I am leaving behind	I am moving toward
fear and anxiety	freedom in Christ
Satan's foothold in my life	my King
comparing myself to others	joyfully giving more of myself
insecurity	meeting others' needs around me
what others think	allowing God to transform lives using my gifts
holding back	boldness
shame and exhaustion	running my race
comfort	faith
discouragement	complete surrender
being paralyzed	fulfillment in God's purpose for me
my shallow faith	depth with Jesus
easy comfort	Jesus and others
judgment	having faith in what God can do, and just doing it
control	obedience and trust
fear	whatever is ahead of time
worrying that God wasn't calling me	recruiting more leaders to run together to Christ
rules that shackle	freedom
insecurity	wild abandon
apathy	intentionality
restlessness	doing something (fix your eyes on Jesus and move)
busyness	listening
discouragement	absolute trust
guilt	freedom
approval	Jesus and where the Holy Spirit leads
fear	facing the unknown with the One who does know
muddy dreams	needs of people right in front of me
restlessness	dreaming big
this world	eternity

ACKNOWLEDGMENTS

There is an order to this type of thing: first God and then family and so on. But as you know, this project was built around moments that life changed forever because of Sarah Henry.

Sarah, you have changed everything about life. It can't go back for you, and it will never go back for us. We have watched you face death and days worse than death, and you still glow with a faith that transcends any earthly understanding.

There must be a God, because instead of shaking your fist, you have taught me to trust and love him more. You are brave, and I want to lean into the story God has for me the way you have mighty friend.

I love you.

Now to the others:

God, what a lovely sense of humor you have. I fight you, unsure every moment, and yet through the pain of it all, you give me what I need. Thank you for allowing me to be a little part of your story. You have the best, greatest story that could ever be imagined and it is an honor to build with you for it.

Zac, my love, thank you for being a man who pushes me to

dream and obey. I love your sacrifice and protection of me. God gave me the best teammate on earth. You run faster than me, and yet you never leave me behind. I love you so.

To my kids: as I watch the threads of your lives begin to come together for great purposes, I want you to know we admire you so. You, my tribe of little awesome people, will change the world.

Conner, somewhere in the midst of these words you became a young man, and I love the man you are becoming. Your passion and strength are contagious and you light up our family with your mop of blond hair and sinister smile. I am proud that you are my son; and with your sharp mind, you will build great things so others prosper. I can't wait to see how.

Kate, you just get it. You get God and people and compassion in the deepest places in your soul. You crave all the right things: mercy and more of God and loving people. All of that mixed with your way with words and creativity will come together to impact people's souls. I see your threads, and they are already building the best stories.

Caroline, I love that pajamas and cuddling are enough for you to be happy every day. You bring a passionate joy to our home; you won't let us all miss each other. You are only eight, and you are one of the hardest workers I know. I think it is because you love beauty—the kind of beauty that comes from tables set with cloth napkins. You are winsome and kind, and many will want your God because of the way you love and serve.

Cooper, at six years old no one wonders if you will change the world. You will. You have. You charge into a room, into our lives, with authority and direction. There are no strangers, and your curiosity causes us all to wonder at God. You are a leader, and I envision the many lives that the threads of your story will impact.

And to the women who went to the hard places with me as *Restless* was taking shape in Austin: you made me believe God could use this work, these words. You were brave, and you live beautiful lives with unique threads. Thank you for investing in this with me.

To the friends in Austin who became sisters this year, thank you for cheering and praying and speaking life into my weary bones. I don't remember life without our text-stream sisterhood. And to Annie Downs: you made me believe I could write on empty and that God would come through. Love you forever.

Many of these words were processed and written in a space that Cecil Eager graciously carved out for me. Cecil runs the Gruene Mansion Inn, a bed and breakfast in Gruene, Texas. And after many long, lonely nights of writing in the most ideal little writing cabin an hour from home, I would walk in for an obscene feast of a breakfast and he would be there with his warm smile and coffee and he would sit with me. Because that is what he does in Gruene. Cecil, your lifetime of threads have woven into a beautiful story and calling. Everything about the space you have created slows the soul.

I needed my soul to slow so that I could write these words. So readers, if you ever stop by this heavenly place, be sure to thank him for me.

And to the teams of people who believed in this enough to give their time and money and hearts to it, thank you. Curtis Yates, I can't imagine how much time you have spent on me in our brief relationship. Thank you for taking me on. I know you now feel brave for such an endeavor! Thank you for always thinking I am crazy and then helping me be crazy anyway. You are much more than an agent—you and Karen are dear friends.

Debbie Wickwire, you lose sleep with me over these words. You remind me why we all do this, and you show me God—and feel more like family than an editor. Thank you. To Matt Baugher, Adria Haley, Jennifer McNeil, Emily Sweeney, Stephanie Newton, Pamela McClure, Jana Muntsinger, John Raymond, Robin Phillips, Mark Weising, Chris Fann, and the countless others who broke molds with me and gave too much time to this project, your threads are as much a part of shaping this as mine. Thank you for believing in me and in this. Wouldn't it be fun if God took these efforts and unleashed people to his purposes on earth? I pray he does, and I hope you feel a big part of it!

I am blessed.

NOTES

Chapter 3: Die to Live

1. Todd Harper, "Our Contract with God: An Interview with Bill and Vonette Bright," Generous Giving Website, http://library.generousgiving.org/articles/display.asp?id=123.
2. 1 Cor. 6:20; Gal. 2:20.
3. Jennie Allen, *Anything* (Nashville: Thomas Nelson, 2011), 105–06.
4. Jennie Allen (blog), "When It Feels Like God Forgot," December 20, 2012, http://jennieallen.com/blog/when-it-feels-like-god-forgot/.

Chapter 4: Permission to Dream

1. Merriam-Webster Online, s.v. "dream," accessed May 30, 2013, http://www.merriam-webster.com/dictionary/dream.
2. Claude-Michel Schonberg (music), Alain Boublil, Jean-Marc Natel, Herbert Kretzmer (lyrics), "I Dreamed a Dream," *Les Miserables* (film), Universal Pictures, 2012.

Chapter 5: Uncertainties

1. Kevin DeYoung, *Just Do Something* (Chicago: Moody Publishers, 2009).

2. John Piper, "How Can I Discern the Specific Calling of God on My Life?" Desiring God (blog), November 14, 2007, http://www.desiringgod.org/resource-library/ask-pastor-john /how-can-i-discern-the-specific-calling-of-god-on-my-life.
3. Col. 3:23.

Chapter 6: Pleasing God

1. Gen. 11.
2. Ex. 3:7–8 paraphrased, emphasis added.
3. Timothy Keller, *Every Good Endeavor* (New York: Dutton, 2012).
4. Daniel Radcliffe, interview on *Larry King Live*, CNN, July 10, 2011.

Chapter 8: The Process

1. Timothy Keller, *Every Good Endeavor* (New York: Dutton, 2012).
2. Matt. 15:34 paraphrased.
3. Often attributed to Mark Twain. In H. Jackson Brown, *P.S. I Love You* (Nashville: Rutledge Hill, 1990), 13.

Chapter 10: The Immovable Fabric

1. Gen. 1:26.
2. Gen. 1:27 paraphrased.
3. Gen. 6:5 paraphrased.
4. John 1:12.
5. 1 Cor. 2:9.
6. 2 Cor. 5:5.
7. 2 Tim. 3:17.
8. Heb. 10:37 ESV.
9. Rev. 12:10 paraphrased.
10. Rev. 12:11 paraphrased.
11. Psalm 118:1 ESV.
12. Heb. 10:37.
13. C. S. Lewis, *The Last Battle* (New York: Harper Collins, 2009), 228.

Chapter 11: The Starting Place

1. Brennan Manning, *Abba's Child*, expanded ed. (Colorado Springs: NavPress, 2002), 29, 105.
2. Matt Redman, "10,000 Reasons," *10,000 Reasons* (Sparrow Records: 2011).

Chapter 12: Threads of Gifts

1. Hugh Hudson, director, *Chariots of Fire* (Enigma Productions, 1981).

Chapter 13: Threads of Suffering

1. Mary Beth Chapman, interview (paraphrased) on *Good Morning America*, ABC, December 14, 2009.
2. Isa. 61:3 paraphrased.
3. Gen. 50:20 paraphrased.
4. Gilbert Tuhabonye and Gary Brozek, *The Voice in My Heart* (New York: HarperCollins, 2006), 206.

Chapter 14: Threads of Places

1. Jim Elliot, as quoted by Elisabeth Elliot, *Through Gates of Splendor* (Peabody, MA: Hendrickson Publishers, 1956, 1996), 11.

Chapter 15: Threads of People

1. Gen. 50:20 paraphrased.

Chapter 16: Threads of Passions

1. Eric Metaxas, *Amazing Grace* (New York: HarperCollins, 2007).
2. Michel Apted, director, *Amazing Grace* (20th Century Fox, 2007).
3. Frederick Buechner, *Wishful Thinking* (New York: HarperOne, 1993).

Chapter 17: The Tailor

1. Merriam-Webster Online, s.v. "regenerate," accessed June 4, 2013, http://www.merriam-webster.com/dictionary/regenerate.
2. Prov. 3:6 paraphrased.

Chapter 20: Shrinking Back

1. Steven Pressfield, *The War of Art* (New York: Black Irish Entertainment, 2002).
2. Luke 22:42 paraphrased.
3. 1 Cor. 10:23 paraphrased.

Chapter 21: When Women Dream

1. Gal. 3:28.

Chapter 22: Focused and Steady

1. Bill Gates, *The Road Ahead* (New York: Penguin, 1996), 316.

Chapter 23: The End of the Mundane

1. C. S. Lewis, *The Weight of Glory* (New York: HarperOne, 1949, 2001), 39.

How to Find God

1. Augustine of Hippo, *Saint Augustine's Confessions*, trans. Albert C. Outler (Mineola: Courier Dover Publications: 2002), 103.

ABOUT THE AUTHOR

JENNIE ALLEN is a passionate leader and visionary following God's call to inspire a new generation of women to encounter the invisible God. With a Master's in Biblical Studies from DTS, Jennie is the author of two Bible studies, *Stuck*, a CBA best-seller, and *Chase*, and the ECPA "New Author of the Year" winner of *Anything* and *Restless*, which also includes a video-based Bible study of the same name. Jennie is the founder of IF: Gathering. She lives in Austin, Texas, is married to her best friend, Zac, and has been blessed with four children, the youngest of whom was adopted from Rwanda.

Also Available from
jennie allen

Identify the threads of your life

In this DVD-based study using the story of Joseph, Jennie explains how his suffering, gifts, story, and relationships fit into the greater story of God—and how your story can do the same. She introduces Threads—a tool to help you see your own personal story and to uncover and understand the raw materials God has given you to use for his glory and purpose.

Visit **www.jennieallen.com** for info about *Restless*.

Available wherever books & Bibles are sold.

Also Available from
jennie allen

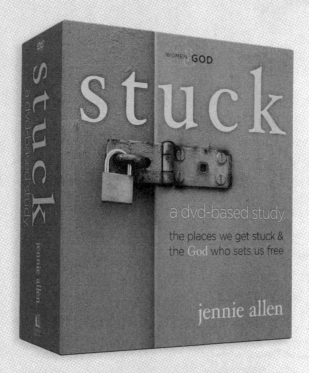

A New Bible Study Experience for Women

Women are hurting. A lot of us feel stuck. This is not a novel perception—this is human. We are stuck trying to be perfect. Stuck in sadness. Stuck feeling numb. Stuck pursuing more stuff to make us happy. Stuck in something we can't even name. *Stuck* is an eight-session Bible study experience leading women to the invisible struggles that we fi ght and to the God who has to set us free.

Visit **www.stuckdvdstudy.com** to learn more.

Available wherever books & Bibles are sold.

Also Available from
jennie allen

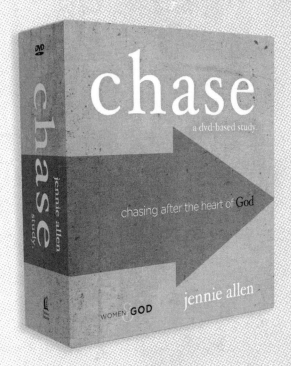

Chasing After the Heart of God

Chase is a Bible study experience to discover the heart of God and what it is exactly He wants from us. As we work through major events in the life of David, and the Psalms he wrote out of those experiences, you see a man who was reckless and imperfect but possessed the favor of God. Whether you are running from God or working your tail off to please Him, this man's journey will challenge your view of God.

Watch **www.jennieallen.com** for more info about *Chase*.

Available wherever books & Bibles are sold.

Also Available from
jennie allen

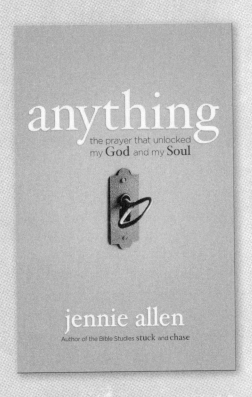

What if you told God you would do anything . . . and he took you up on it?

Bible teacher Jennie Allen wrestles with the questions we face as we hand our lives over to a living, unpredictable, invisible God. She introduces readers to the enemies of surrender, leading them to face the minefields of unbelief, entitlement, control, and fear. With a fresh voice and bold vulnerability, Jennie helps shatter our small view of God as she shares her own story of wrestling to surrender.

W PUBLISHING GROUP

I F : G A T H E R I N G

GATHER
EQUIP
UNLEASH

IFGATHERING.COM